U.S. Department
of Transportation

**National Highway
Traffic Safety
Administration**

Evaluation of Child Occupant Protection
In a 56 km/h (35 MPH) Frontal Barrier Crash

Technical Report
May 2005

U.S. Department
of Transportation

**National Highway
Traffic Safety
Administration**

Memorandum

Subject:	**Action**: Submission of Technical Report titled "Evaluation of Child Occupant Protection in a 56 KPH (35MPH) Frontal Barrier Crash"
From:	Brian Park New Car Assessment Program
To:	Docket Number: NHTSA-2004-18682

Date:

Reply to Attn. of:

5/17/05

THRU: Nathaniel Beuse
Division Chief, New Car Assessment Program

Roger A. Saul
Director, Office of Crashworthiness Standards

Jacqueline Glassman
Chief Counsel

Please submit the attached technical report titled "Evaluation of Child Occupant Protection in a 56 KPH (35MPH) Frontal Barrier Crash " to NHTSA Docket 2004-18682. This report is a summary of child dummy data obtained from MY 2001 to 2004 vehicle testing conducted under the New Car Assessment Program. Data from these tests are located in docket NHTSA-1999-4962.

Attachment
"Evaluation of Child Occupant Protection in a 56 KPH (35MPH) Frontal Barrier Crash"

Get it together!

SAFETY BELTS SAVE LIVES

Table of Contents

TECHNICAL REPORT DOCUMENTATION PAGE..1

I.   BACKGROUND 2

II. TESTS METHODOLOGY..2

    A.   Injury Assessment...3

    B.   Test Setup...4

    C.   Experimental Design...4

        1. 2001 CRS Study...4

        2. 2002 CRS Study...4

        3. 2003 CRS Study...5

        4. 2004 CRS Study...6

    D.   Statistical Analysis 6

III. TEST RESULTS & DISCUSSION 6

    A.   Forward-Facing Vs. Rear-Facing – One-Year-Old vs. Three-Year-Old 6

    B.   Forward-Facing Vs. Booster – Three-Year-Old vs. Six-Year-Old 7

    C.   One-Year-Old – Infant CRS vs. Convertible CRS...8

    *D.   Three-Year-Old Forward-Facing Five-Point Harness vs. Three-Year-Old
        Overhead Shield* 9*

    E.   Comparison Between Different Brand Child Restraints in the Same Vehicle 9

    F.   Comparison Between Economical and Higher Priced CRS 10

    G.   50th Percentile Injury Results vs. Three-Year-Old Injury Results....................10

    H.   Vehicle Type vs. CRS Performance..11

    I.   Vehicle Crash Pulse 12

IV. CONCLUSIONS 12

FIGURES 14

APPENDIX 31

Figures

Figure 1: Evenflo Vanguard V Compliance Test 15
Figure 2: Normalized HIC Values for Paired Tests 16
Figure 3: Normalized Chest G Values for Paired Tests.. 17
Figure 4: Normalized Chest G Values for Paired Tests.. 18
Figure 5: Normalized HIC Values for Paired Comparison... 19
Figure 6: Results for Rear-Facing Infant and Rear-Facing Convertible Restraints 20
Figure 7: Normalized HIC Values for Paired Tests 21
Figure 8: Normalized Chest G Values for Paired Tests.. 22
Figure 9: Normalized HIC Values for Paired Comparison... 23
Figure 10: Normalized Chest G Values for Paired Tests.. 24
Figure 11: HIC Comparison Between Three-Year-Old and 50th-percentile 25
Figure 12: Chest G Comparison Between Three-Year-Old and 50th-percentile 26
Figure 13: Three-Year-Old Injury Data Plotted by Vehicle Type 27
Figure 14: Chest G vs. Crash Pulse Peak Acceleration 28
Figure 15: Chest G vs. Vehicle Crash Pulse Duration... 29
Figure 16: Chest G vs. Static Crush Measurement 30

Tables

Table 1: Child Dummy Specifications.. 32
Table 2: 2001 CRS Test Matrix 32
Table 3: 2002 CRS Test Matrix 33
Table 4: 2003 CRS Test Matrix 34
Table 5: Comparison between Vanguard 5 and Roundabout 35
Table 6: Child Dummy Injury Readings for 2001-2004... 38

TECHNICAL REPORT DOCUMENTATION PAGE

1. Report No. 2003-01	2. Government Accession No.	3. Recipients Catalog No.

4. Title and Subtitle	5. Report Date
Evaluation of Child Occupant Protection In a 56 km/h (35 MPH) Frontal Barrier Crash	May 17, 2005
	6. Performing Organization Code NVS-111

7. Author(s) Brian Park, Jesse Swanson, and Taryn Rockwell	8. Performing Organization Report No.

9. Performing Organization Name and Address	10. Work Unit No.
U.S. Department of Transportation	
National Highway Traffic Safety Administration	11. Contract or Grant No.
Rulemaking Office of Crashworthiness Standards	DTNH22-01-C-02047

12. Sponsoring Agency Name and Address	13. Type of Report and Period Covered
U.S. Department of Transportation	
National Highway Traffic Safety Administration	
Rulemaking	Final Report
Office of Crashworthiness Standards Mail Code: NVS-111 400 Seventh Street, SW, Room 5307 Washington, D.C. 20590	14. Sponsoring Agency Code NHTSA

15. Supplementary Notes

16. Abstract

In response to the TREAD Act, the agency added child restraints to the rear seat of several frontal crash tests in 2001 and 2002, and in most frontal crash test for 2003 and 2004 conducted under the New Car Assessment Program (NCAP). Child dummies representing one, three, and six-year-old children were placed in various child restraints, including rear-facing, forward-facing, and booster seats. Tests with the Hybrid III three-year-old showed little variance between different child restraints tested in the same vehicle, but showed significantly greater variance in tests with the same restraint, but different vehicle. Vehicle type had little correlation with test results. Analyses also showed that the Hybrid III three-year-old had a statistically significant better chest G performance than either the CRABI one-year-old and Hybrid III six-year-old dummies. Analysis did not indicate a statistically significant HIC performance difference between the Hybrid III three-year-old and either the CRABI one-year-old or the Hybrid III six-year-old, however, the Hybrid III three-year-old dummy tended to have better HIC performance than the Hybrid III six-year-old dummy. In addition, limited analysis showed a rear-facing CRS that interacts with the front seat tends to result in higher chest readings in the dummy.

17. Key Words	18. Distribution Statement
New Car Assessment Program (NCAP) Frontal Impact Child Restraint System (CRS) Child Occupant Protection	Copies of this report are available from: National Highway Traffic Safety Admin. NHTSA Technical Reference Division 400 Seventh St., SW, Room 5108 Washington, DC 20590

19. Security Classification (of this report) UNCLASSIFIED	20. Security Classification (of this page) UNCLASSIFIED	21. No. of Pages 46	22. Price

I. BACKGROUND

On November 1, 2000, Congress passed the Transportation Recall Enhancement, Accountability, and Documentation (TREAD) Act, Public Law 106-414 (114 Stat. 1800). Under that Act, the Secretary of Transportation was required to develop a child restraint safety rating that was practicable and understandable (Section 14 g) in order to help consumers make an informed decision in the purchase of a child restraint. In addition, Section 14(b)(9) of the TREAD Act required consideration for placing child restraint systems (CRS) in the rear seats of vehicles being crash tested under the New Car Assessment Program (NCAP).

The National Highway Traffic Safety Administration (NHTSA) considers that child restraints are highly effective in reducing the likelihood of death and/or serious injury in motor vehicle crashes. In the latest study, NHTSA estimated that for children younger than one year, a child restraint could reduce the risk of fatality by 71 percent when used in a passenger car and by 58 percent when used in a pickup truck, van, or sport utility vehicle (light truck)[1]. The agency is also aware that the lack of occupant restraint use by motorists is a significant factor in most fatalities resulting from motor vehicle crashes.

In 2001, NHTSA initiated a study by including child restraints and child dummies in frontal NCAP crash tests. Although not all 2001 frontal NCAP tests had child restraints, NCAP tested 20 vehicles in frontal crash tests with a Hybrid III three-year-old (3YO) dummy and forward-facing child restraints. NHTSA expanded the study in 2002 to include rear-facing child restraints with the child restraint airbag interaction (CRABI) one-year-old (1YO) dummy.

In response to Section 14 g, the NHTSA published a Final Rule on November 6, 2002, establishing a child restraint Ease of Use ratings program, and announced its intent to conduct two, two-year pilot programs to gather additional information on child safety. NHTSA intends that one pilot program would investigate the feasibility of a rating based on a child restraint's dynamic performance. This would be accomplished by conducting sled tests on subject child restraints positioned in various configurations and occupied by dummies of various sizes. The second pilot program would investigate the feasibility of rating vehicles on how well they protect children by installing child restraints in the rear seats of vehicles tested in the existing frontal NCAP. The two-year pilot program was tested through Model Year (MY) 2003 and 2004 frontal NCAP tests. Vehicles tested under frontal NCAP that were equipped with a rear seat had at least one child restraint positioned in the rear seat. This report will summarize and analyze the data from all 35 mph full frontal NCAP vehicle tests conducted by the agency with child restraints in the rear seats.

II. TESTS METHODOLOGY

Since 1979, the agency has used NCAP to evaluate the frontal crashworthiness performance of new vehicles using test procedures derived from Federal Motor Vehicle

---

[1] Report to Congress: Child Restraint Systems, Transportation Recall Enhancement, Accountability, and Documentation (TREAD) Act, February 2004

Safety Standard Number 208 (FMVSS No. 208), "Occupant Crash Protection". In recent years, NCAP has been able to conduct a full-frontal rigid barrier test on approximately 30-40 new vehicles each model year. For the frontal crash, the agency performs these tests by positioning two 50th percentile adult dummies in the front seat, and historically, no occupants in the vehicles' rear seats. However, in response to the TREAD Act, NCAP has begun to add child restraints to these frontal crash tests to study the protection offered to child occupants in these severe frontal collisions.

To date, NCAP has used the CRABI one-year-old, the Hybrid III three-year-old, and the Hybrid III six-year-old (6YO) dummies to study child protection in frontal vehicle crashes. The Hybrid III family of dummies is considered to be more biofidelic than the previous Hybrid II child dummies. In addition to measuring head acceleration and chest acceleration, each Hybrid III dummy has an instrumented neck that is capable of measuring shear, extension, and compression forces, as well as flexion and extension moments. Physical characteristics of each dummy are tabulated in Table 1 of the Appendix A.

A. *Injury Assessment*

Currently, NCAP uses the Head Injury Criterion (HIC) to assess the probability of a head injury and the chest acceleration (chest G) to evaluate the probability of a chest injury. HIC is determined using the resultant acceleration at the center of gravity of the head. HIC can be calculated for any time interval (HIC unwindowed; HIC uw), or a maximum time interval can be established. This was done with the latest upgrade to FMVSS No. 213, which limits the time interval to 36 milliseconds (HIC 36). HIC uw is always equal to or greater than HIC 36.[2] The chest acceleration is measured in Gs, where 1 G is approximately 9.8 m/s^2 (32.2 ft/s^2). The maximum value for chest acceleration is calculated over a three-millisecond duration.

The injury assessment reference values (IARVs) published in the June 23, 2003 upgrade to FMVSS No. 213 "Child Restraint Systems," were used to evaluate and normalize all of the child dummy data. These IARVs are HIC 36 of 1000 and chest acceleration of 60. Neck and pelvis data is also available in the individual test reports for these tests[3], but results will not be presented in this report since FMVSS No. 213 does not set limits for those measurements.

In addition to processing the child dummy data obtained from the tests to obtain the IARVs mentioned, film analysis and a thorough physical examination of the child restraints were done post-test. After each vehicle crash test, the testing facilities examined the child restraint for structural integrity using the laboratory procedures outlined for FMVSS No. 213[4].

---

[2] Docket No. NHTSA-03-15351
[3] Docket Number 10053
[4] TP-213-04 (10 December 1997)

B. *Test Setup*

The test procedure used by frontal NCAP is based on the belted dynamic vehicle crash test of FMVSS No. 208. The procedure for FMVSS No. 208 was based on years of NHTSA developmental work, with input from the automotive industry and safety advocates.[5] The major difference between FMVSS No. 208 and the frontal NCAP is the test speed. NCAP conducts its frontal crashes at 56 KMPH (35 MPH) compared to the current FMVSS No. 208 standard, which crashes the vehicles at 48 KMPH (30 MPH). Both NCAP and FMVSS No. 208 tow a vehicle into an instrumented, fixed rigid barrier and measure the response recorded by the test dummies. The frontal NCAP laboratory procedures were used to setup the vehicles that were to be tested for this pilot program, and the child restraint manufacturers instructions were used child restraint installation. These documents ensured that child restraints would be properly installed in the vehicles across all test facilities that perform frontal crash tests. For every test, a certified child restraint technician installed the child restraints. The child dummies had chalk painted to their head, knees, and feet to determine if these parts made contact with the vehicle interior or other parts of the dummy and/or child restraint during the test.

C. *Experimental Design*

Since MY 2001, NCAP has studied the performance of various types of child restraints in various vehicle types. During MY 2001 and MY 2002, due to a limited budget, NCAP was not able to incorporate child restraints in every frontal vehicle test. However, in MY 2003 and 2004, NCAP was able to place at least one child restraint in every frontal crash test vehicle equipped with a rear seat. In these studies, NHTSA's main focus was evaluating (1) the variance of a single child restraint's performance in various vehicle types and sizes, (2) the child restraint and vehicle interaction, and (3) the performance of different child restraints in the same vehicle.

1. 2001 CRS Study

In support of the TREAD Act, the agency first incorporated child restraints into the rear seats of twenty frontal NCAP vehicles to be crash-tested during the MY 2001 testing program. In this initial study, the agency evaluated the Hybrid III three-year old dummy in six different five-point, forward-facing child restraints. These child restraints were installed with the Lower Anchors and Tethers for Children (LATCH), or the vehicle seat belts and the top tether. Table 2 of the Appendix A shows the test matrix for the 2001 study.

2. 2002 CRS Study

In 2002, the agency continued incorporating child restraints into the frontal vehicle crash tests, but due to agency priorities, NCAP was only able to incorporate child restraints into ten vehicles. In addition, because the previous year's study examined the performance of the Hybrid III three-year-old child dummy in forward-facing restraints, it was of interest to examine the performance of rear-facing child restraints and the CRABI one-year-old dummy. Because these restraints were rear-facing, only the lower anchorages of the

---

[5] Federal Register 49 (17 July 1984): 28962. Also Code of Federal Regulations, Title 49, Part 571.208, General Printing Office, Washington, 1992.

LATCH system were used. Table 3 of Appendix A shows the test matrix for the 2002 study.

3. 2003 CRS Study

The MY 2003 test series involved placing at least one child restraint in every frontal NCAP vehicle crash test, for a total 33 tests. Given the limited number of tests, and after careful review of agency data that had already been collected from the MY 2001 and MY 2002 testing, the agency decided to gather statistically comparable information on the following: (1) forward-facing five-point harness child restraints vs. rear-facing child restraints, (2) forward-facing five-point harness restraints vs. booster seats, and (3) forward-facing five-point harness child restraints vs. forward-facing overhead shield restraints. At least eight samples for each comparison were collected in order to perform statistical analysis.

Unlike the MY 2001 and MY 2002 testing, most vehicles tested in the MY 2003 frontal NCAP had two child restraints in the rear seating positions. All child restraints were installed using LATCH. For rear-facing child restraints, only the lower anchorages were used to secure the child restraint. In the seating position behind the front seat passenger (P3), the same CRS (baseline CRS) and the Hybrid III three-year old child dummy were positioned in every vehicle, while the CRS and child dummy used in the seating position behind the driver (P4) was varied to gather information on additional child restraints and child dummies and to serve as a comparison for the baseline CRS.

The selection of the baseline CRS was based on the restraint's performance in the FMVSS No. 213 compliance test, the restraint's cost, and its popularity. Head injury criterion and chest acceleration were used to evaluate the restraint's performance in the dynamic test environment. These injury readings were plotted for all upright and reclined, tethered, convertible (five-point and overhead shield) child restraints subjected to the FMVSS No. 213 compliance testing from 2000-2003. Upon analysis of the 213 compliance test results, shown in Figure 1, the Evenflo Vanguard V convertible child restraint was selected because its performance in the test was representative of other convertible child restraints tested that year. Convertible child restraints range in cost from as little as $50 to over $250. The Vanguard V is a mid-priced restraint, costing about $80 and thus making it widely available. In addition, according to conversations with several retailers of child restraints, the Vanguard V is a popular choice of restraint for many consumers. Furthermore, because one goal of the 2003 study was to evaluate overhead shield restraints, the Vanguard V uses the same shell as the Evenflo Vanguard Comfort, which is an overhead shield. In this way, the same restraint, equipped with a different harness, could be compared.

Depending on the particular test, the seat behind the driver contained either a different child restraint and/or child dummy, or the Vanguard V positioned in the rear-facing mode with the CRABI dummy. The restraints chosen for this position were selected based on their performance in the 213 test, availability, popularity, and price. Table 4 in the Appendix A shows the test matrix for 2003.

4. 2004 CRS Study

The MY 2004 NCAP test series was similar to the previous year in that every vehicle with a rear seat was tested with at least one child restraint. NHTSA tested 43 MY 2004 vehicles with child restraints. The main focus of the 2004 tests was to compare one convertible CRS to another model within the same vehicle. These tests utilized the three-year old in an Evenflo Vanguard 5 in the P3 position and various other models in the P4 position.

Eleven of the tests compared the moderately priced Evenflo Vanguard 5 to the higher priced Britax Roundabout. It was of interest to see if a higher priced CRS offered additional occupant protection compared to its economical competitor.

D. *Statistical Analysis*

The MY 2003 and 2004 NCAP test matrix was designed so that comparisons could be made with statistical confidence. Given the large number of vehicle-CRS combinations and the limited number of tests, it was important to test as many combinations as possible, yet have a large enough sample to make statistically sound conclusions. Typically, it is difficult to determine if differences based on a small number of tests are statistically significant. One method for dealing with small sample size is the use of paired tests. The statistical significance of observed differences was determined using a paired t-test and a Wilcoxon signed rank test. Paired tests, in this case two seats in the same vehicle, enable one to implicitly control for factors other than performance differences. Since the left and right positions of the rear seat are mirror images of each other, it was assumed that the performance is independent of the position.

Using this information and based on the number of vehicles, it was determined that a minimum of eight samples would be adequate for statistically significant comparisons. This allowed for NCAP to make three detailed comparisons. These three comparisons were: (1) the performance differences between the Hybrid III three-year-old and the CRABI one-year-old, (2) the performance differences between the Hybrid III three-year-old and the Hybrid III six-year-old, and (3) the differences between the performance of the five-point harness and the overhead shield.

III. TEST RESULTS & DISCUSSION

A. *Forward-Facing Vs. Rear-Facing – One-Year-Old vs. Three-Year-Old*

The CRABI one-year-old dummy and the Hybrid III three-year-old dummy were paired in eight vehicle tests in MY 2003 vehicles. The CRABI dummy was positioned rear-facing and the Hybrid III three-year-old dummy was positioned forward-facing. Head and chest data for the Hybrid III three-year-old and the CRABI one-year-old is available for all tests. All vehicles used the Vanguard V child restraint for both child dummies.

As shown in Figure 2, the dummies generally recorded different levels of HIC 36 injury in each test. In four tests, the Hybrid III three-year-old dummy recorded greater HIC 36 readings than the CRABI dummy, and in the other four tests, the CRABI dummy measured greater readings than the Hybrid III three-year-old dummy. On average, the difference between the normalized HIC reading for the Hybrid III three-year-old and the CRABI was only 0.06. This difference did not achieve statistical significance.

In addition to examining the HIC, the crash film and the post-test pictures were analyzed. Both the film analysis and the post-test pictures indicated that in some of the tests, the front seat interacted with the Vanguard V child restraint in the rear-facing mode. The CRS in the Mercedes C Class, Mazda 6, and Jaguar X-type was in contact with the front seatback prior to testing. Even though each of these restraints was properly positioned in accordance with the CRS manufacturer's instructions, these restraints all interacted with the front seatback. The Mercedes C Class and Jaguar X-type recorded the two highest HIC values of the eight CRABI tests. However, interaction did not always result in a relatively high HIC. The Mazda 6, which had front seat interaction, had a normalized HIC of 0.51 for the CRABI dummy. During the Mazda 6 pretest set up, the child restraint interacted with the front seatback, but during the test, the front seat rotated forward allowing the child restraint to rotate as well.

A comparison of chest acceleration readings for the CRABI dummy and the Hybrid III three-year-old dummy, shown in Figure 3, indicate that in seven of the eight test vehicles, the CRABI one-year-old dummy recorded higher chest acceleration than the Hybrid III three-year-old dummy. The average difference between the normalized chest acceleration for the CRABI and the Hybrid III three-year-old was 0.14, and this difference was statistically significant at the 0.05-level. However, the difference across the dummies could be the result of the front seat interaction with the CRABI in the rear-facing seat. The Mercedes C Class and the Jaguar X-type recorded the highest chest acceleration values of the eight CRABI tests, and both exceeded the IARV of 60 G. The Mazda 6, the third vehicle with front seat interaction, recorded the fourth highest value. Furthermore, film analysis of the Mercedes C Class crash event showed that the CRS interacting with the front seat likely caused the high acceleration.

B. *Forward-Facing Vs. Booster – Three-Year-Old vs. Six-Year-Old*

The booster seat is a unique child restraint that relies solely on the vehicles' seat belts to restrain the child occupant. In this comparison study, eleven vehicles were tested with both a Hybrid III six-year-old and a Hybrid III three-year-old child dummy. The Hybrid III six-year-old dummy was restrained in the Graco My CarGo booster seat and the Hybrid III three-year-old dummy was restrained forward-facing in the Vanguard V convertible child restraint. Figure 4 shows the chest acceleration for all eleven vehicles. The average difference between the normalized chest acceleration for the Hybrid III six-year-old and for the Hybrid III three-year-old was 0.1, and this difference achieved statistical significance at the 0.10-level using both a paired t-test and Wilcoxon signed rank test. However, a similar conclusion could not be made for HIC 36. Although, Figure 5 shows that in eight of the eleven tests, the Hybrid III six-year-old dummy did record higher HIC 36 readings than the Hybrid III three-year-old dummy, the average difference in the normalized HIC value between the Hybrid III six-year-old and the Hybrid III three-year-old of 0.53 was not statistically significant. The lack of statistical significance is due to in large part to the Volvo XC90 test results where, unlike the other tests, the Hybrid III three-year-old experienced a much higher HIC value than the Hybrid

III six-year-old. Removing the Volvo XC90 test leads to statistically significant higher HIC values for the Hybrid III six-year-old than the Hybrid III three-year-old.

Additionally, it should be noted that the Hybrid III six-year-old dummy's face contacted its chest in every test. In half of the tests the face-to-chest contact occurred during the HIC 36 calculation. That is, a small spike could be seen in the 36-millisecond window. Using film analysis, one could determine that the contact caused the spike. However, by artificially removing the spike and recalculating the HIC, analysis showed that this spike only had a small influence on the HIC value. A more detailed analysis is available in Appendix A. For chest acceleration, the contact did not have any bearing on the 3ms chest acceleration calculation.

C. One-Year-Old – Infant CRS vs. Convertible CRS

In MY 2002, infant restraints were tested in a total of 4 vehicles. Although infant restraints were not paired in the same vehicle, like convertible restraints in the rear-facing mode, it was of interest to see if any generalizations could be made. Examining the injury values in Figure 6, both the HIC 36 and chest acceleration injury readings recorded by the CRABI one-year-old dummy were similar for both infant child restraints and convertible child restraints, when positioned in the rear-facing mode. There are too few data points to determine if statistically significant differences exist. In general, however, the dummy injury readings appear to have a similar distribution regardless of whether the child restraint was a convertible restraint or an infant restraint.

Both rear-facing convertible restraints and infant restraints interacted with the back of the front seat in several tests. Because of the limited number of tests for infant restraints, it is difficult to say whether a rear-facing convertible restraint, which tends to be larger than an infant restraint, and thus is positioned closer to the back of the front seat on average, may be more likely to interact with the front seatback, and thereby result in higher injury values. For example, two rear-facing convertible restraints did interact with the front seatback and had the highest dummy injury readings. Two additional rear-facing convertible restraints interacted with the front seatback and produced particularly large chest acceleration measures. Two infant restraints interacted with the front seatback as well and had higher injury readings. The infant seat in the 2002 Toyota Camry interacted with the front seatback, causing a HIC 36 injury reading of 933 and a chest acceleration reading of 58. The infant seat in the 2002 Legacy also showed interaction with the front seatback yielding a chest acceleration reading of 59 and a HIC 36 reading of 592. Overall, half of the tests involving each type of seat interacted with the front seatback. Therefore, it cannot be concluded at this time whether or not the size of the child restraint in rear-facing mode may affect the injury numbers. However, the data seems to indicate that front seatback interaction, in general, tends to induce higher dummy injury readings. Whether this interaction is due to the rearward movement of the front seat back itself or to the size, and thus the relative position of the child restraint, is still to be determined.

D. *Three-Year-Old Forward-Facing Five-Point Harness vs. Three-Year-Old Overhead Shield*

It was also of interest to examine if a Hybrid III three-year-old dummy in a five-point harness or an overhead shield restraint would show similar performance in the forward-facing mode. Eight vehicles were tested with the Hybrid III three-year-old dummy in a five-point harness restraint, positioned in the right rear, paired with a Hybrid III three-year-old in an overhead shield child restraint, positioned in the left rear. The 2003 Nissan Murano was considered anomalous due to the dummy head contacting the dummy knee and was dropped from the analysis. All restraints were oriented to be in the forward-facing mode. The overhead shield model had an identical shell to the five-point model, except that the overhead shield restraint came equipped with a plastic shield covered in cloth and padding and a 3-point harness instead of a five-point harness.

Generally, the HIC 36 readings varied for the two types of restraints, as Figure 7 shows. In six of the eight tests, HIC 36 readings were higher for the Hybrid III three-year-old in the five-point harness restraint than for the same type of dummy in an overhead shield restraint. However, the average differences in the normalized HIC between the five-point harness and overhead shield of 0.09 were not statistically significant. Figure 8 shows similar results for chest acceleration. The average difference in the normalized chest acceleration between the five-point harness and overhead shield of 0.03 was not statistically significant.

E. *Comparison Between Different Brand Child Restraints in the Same Vehicle*

In this comparison, 36 vehicles were tested with an identical child restraint setup; all child restraints were five-point harness restraints, positioned in the forward-facing mode with the Hybrid III three-year-old dummy. The purpose of this comparison was to see if two different five-point harness-type child restraints offered similar performance in the same vehicle. Test results for MY 2001, 2003, and 2004 vehicles were used. The test results for HIC 36 and chest acceleration are shown in Figure 9 and Figure 10, respectively.

An analysis of HIC 36 injury numbers for the Hybrid III three-year-old dummies in the tested vehicles reveals that for any one vehicle, the right rear and left rear passenger child dummies perform similarly, although some variability exists.

Determining the source of difference in child restraint performance was of interest. Variations for HIC and chest acceleration were examined. By comparing the deviation explained by the vehicle make and model (variation across the average value in each vehicle or Model SS) to the total variation (Total SS or Sum of Squared Deviations), the percent of total variation in the HIC and chest acceleration could be determined.

Overall, the child restraint and vehicle make and model explain 88 percent of the variation in chest acceleration and 86 percent of the variation of HIC values. The variation explained is statistically significant at the 0.05 level. However, most of the variance is due to the vehicle make and model when controlling for child restraint. The vehicle make and model explains 64 percent of the variation in chest acceleration values and 63 percent of the variation in HIC values. The variation explained by the vehicle make and model while controlling for the child restraint is statistically significant at the 0.05 level for both HIC and chest acceleration. When controlling for the vehicle make and model, the child restraint model explains approximately 10 percent of the HIC variance and 7 percent of the chest acceleration variance, but does not achieve statistical significance at conventional levels.

These results indicate that when different restraints with the same harness type are placed in the same vehicle, the variation in performance due to vehicle make and model overwhelms the variation due to different restraints. These results do not mean the choice of child restraint does not matter for two reasons. First, the results should be viewed in relative terms. While vehicle make and model produces, and thus explains, more of the test reading variation, a larger set of tests involving more child restraints in the same make and model could indicate a statistically significant effect of seat brand. Second, there is not enough data to test interactions where the performance of the child restraint could depend on the particular vehicle model.

F. *Comparison Between Economical and Higher Priced CRS*

Eleven vehicles were tested with the same two forward-facing child restraints, the Evenflo Vanguard V and the Britax Roundabout. Both restraints were chosen based on cost, popularity, and availability at the time of testing. The average cost of the Vanguard V was about one-third the cost of Roundabout. All tests utilized the Hybrid III three-year-old dummy and the child restraints were secured using LATCH. The results for these tests are shown in Table 5 in Appendix A. For these eleven tests, the injury values were typically lower for the Vanguard V than the Roundabout, suggesting that the cost of a child restraint may have little to do with the level of safety offered by a CRS. In addition, paired t-testing showed that the average difference between the two child restraints is small based upon the injury risk curves. The difference in average HIC response was 58, or a difference of less than 2 percent head injury risk. The difference in average chest acceleration response was 3 G, or about 2 percent difference in chest injury risk. Both t-tests did not achieve statistical significance.

These data suggest that the cost of a child restraint may have little to do with the level of safety offered by the CRS, and that two different child restraints with a five-point harness tested in the same vehicle yield similar test results.

G. *50th Percentile Injury Results vs. Three-Year-Old Injury Results*

Another question these tests were to answer was if similar crash protection was offered to the rear seat occupants compared to the front seat occupants. Injury results from the MY 2003 and 2004 vehicles of the Hybrid III three-year-old dummy, positioned forward-facing in a five-point harness restraint in the right rear passenger position, were compared to those results recorded by the Hybrid III 50th percentile driver and passenger dummies positioned in the front seat, for each corresponding test. These results are shown in Figure 11 and Figure 12. For both HIC 36 and chest acceleration injury results, there does not appear to be a strong relationship between the Hybrid III three-year-old dummy's results and the Hybrid III 50th percentile dummies' results. This finding would indicate that a vehicle that offers good crash protection for the front seat adult occupants might not offer similar protection to the rear seat child passenger occupants. One reason could be that in addition to the seat belts, driver and front passenger protection is supplemented by load limiters, pretensioners, and airbags.

H. *Vehicle Type vs. CRS Performance*

Further evidence that the vehicle make and model affects child restraint performance can be seen by examining the performance of the Hybrid III three-year-old dummy restrained forward-facing in the Vanguard V convertible child restraint. As discussed previously, this configuration was used across 72 vehicle tests as the base case for comparison purposes. If the vehicle make and model did not affect for child restraint performance, then we would expect there to be little variation across the vehicle tests. For the HIC measures, the distribution of cases is as follows: 4 vehicles under 500, 29 vehicles between 500 and 749, 24 vehicles between 750 and 999, 11 vehicles between 1000 and 1499, 3 vehicles between 1500 and 1999, and 1 vehicle between 2000 and 2499. The HIC measures ranged from 366 to 2351, have a mean of 850, and have a standard deviation of 347. For the chest acceleration measures, the distribution of cases is as follows: 9 vehicles between 30 and 39 G, 28 vehicles between 40 and 49 G, 28 vehicles between 50 and 59 G, 6 vehicles between 60 and 69 G and 1 vehicle exceeded 70 G. The chest acceleration measures ranged from 32 to 73 G, have a mean of 49 G, and have a standard deviation of 8 G. The distribution of these HIC and chest acceleration readings indicates that there is large dispersion in the Hybrid III three-year-old readings across vehicles and provide evidence that vehicle make and model can produce large differences in child restraint performance.

While the previous paragraph discussed the dispersion of HIC and chest acceleration readings across vehicles, it did not address what factors account for the variation. This next section considers one possible explanation by examining how child restraint performance varied with the vehicle type. In 2003 and 2004 the same CRS model was tested in different vehicles, and the test results for HIC 36 and chest acceleration for P3 Hybrid III three-year-old dummies are plotted in Figure 13. Vehicles were categorized as cars, Sport Utility Vehicles (SUVs), vans, and pickups. Since only three vans were tested, there was insufficient data to make significant analysis on this vehicle body type. As shown, the data indicates that vehicle type does not appear to affect the performance of child restraints. In other words, although the child dummies in many vehicles had relatively lower HIC 36 and chest acceleration injury numbers than in other MY 2003 vehicles tested, these low injury numbers were not just recorded in one type of vehicle. It can be seen that the right rear child dummy in at least one car, SUV, and pickup truck had low HIC 36 and chest acceleration injury numbers, less than 600 and 40, respectively. But also, a similar observation can be made for higher HIC 36 and chest acceleration injury numbers. The right rear Hybrid III three-year-old dummy in at least one car, SUV, and pickup had a HIC 36 reading greater than 1200 and a chest acceleration injury reading greater than 55 Gs. A statistical analysis using one-way ANOVA also was conducted to explore whether vehicle body type provided a statistically significant explanation of the variation in HIC and chest acceleration values. In neither case did the body type variable achieve statistical significance.

I. *Vehicle Crash Pulse*

To further investigate how much the vehicle influences the results of the child occupant's injury readings, HIC and chest acceleration values were compared with the vehicle crash pulse characteristics. For this comparison, only the Hybrid III three-year-old dummies in the right rear position of the 2003 and 2004 NCAP tests were used. Using the same dummy and child restraint ensures an accurate comparison. Three aspects of the vehicle crash pulse were studied. One was the peak acceleration of the pulse, the second being the duration of the crash pulse, and the third being the amount of crush.

The peak acceleration of the crash pulse was determined from accelerometers located at the rear doorsill or rear floorpan of the vehicle. The peak acceleration was the maximum value recorded after using the Channel Frequency Class 60 filter.[6] Figure 14 shows the chest acceleration values of the dummy compared to the peak acceleration of the crash pulse. This data implies that vehicles with higher peak accelerations would likely show higher chest acceleration values. This correlation had an R^2 value of 0.38 meaning that this one factor explained 38 percent of the variation in chest acceleration values.

The duration of the crash pulse also showed a significant influence on the recorded chest acceleration values. The pulse duration was determined using the same data as the peak acceleration. This data was integrated to determine the amount of time, in milliseconds, for the vehicle to reach zero velocity. This comparison is depicted in Figure 15 and shows that vehicles with longer crash durations will likely produce lower chest acceleration values. This correlation had an R^2 value of 0.62.

One other aspect of the vehicle crush profile that had an influence on chest acceleration was the amount of static crush. This is a static measurement, and unlike peak acceleration and pulse duration, is not recorded by the accelerometers. The crush is determined as the difference of the pretest and posttest measurement of the length of the vehicle. The smaller amounts of crush typically yielded higher chest acceleration values, as can be seen in Figure 16, which had an R^2 value of 0.23.

It is important to realize that other variables that may have an effect but were not recorded during the testing include, but are not limited to, vehicle seat contour, vehicle seat stiffness, seatback angle, and interior space.

IV. CONCLUSIONS

Based upon the results of frontal vehicle crash testing from the MY2001, 2002, 2003 and 2004 NCAP with child restraints in the rear seat, the following observations were made:

- The comparison of rear-facing child restraints with the CRABI one-year-old dummy to the forward-facing child restraints with the Hybrid III three-year-old dummy showed that the CRABI one-year-old did have statistically significant higher chest acceleration, but no conclusion could be made for HIC. However, analysis also showed that the tests where the rear-facing CRS

---

[6] As per SAE J211

interacted with the front seatback tended to be the tests with higher injury measurements for the CRABI one-year-old.

- Comparison of the Hybrid III six-year-old in a belt-positioning booster to the Hybrid III three-year-old in a forward-facing restraint typically showed higher HIC readings and statistically significant higher chest acceleration for the Hybrid III six-year-old.

- Rear-facing infant restraints and rear-facing convertible restraints generally showed similar results for the CRABI one-year-old dummy. During several tests, both types of child restraints had interaction with the front seatback. This interaction typically resulted in higher HIC and chest acceleration readings.

- Evaluations between the five-point harness and the overhead shield for the Hybrid III three-year-old, along with the paired tests with the Hybrid III three-year-old in two different five-point harness child restraints, showed little discrepancy between each pair and indicated differences that were not statistically significant.

- Comparison between an expensive and economical CRS tested in the same vehicle suggest that the price of a CRS may have little to do with the level of safety offered by the CRS. The difference of average HIC and chest acceleration results in a 2 percent difference of head or chest injury.

- A comparison between the HIC and chest acceleration values of the Hybrid III three-year-old in the rear seat to those of the driver and front passenger showed little correlation.

- The paired test results showed no significant difference between the HIC values of the different aged dummies.

- Analysis showed that child restraint and vehicle make and model explain over 88 percent of the variation in chest acceleration and 86 percent of the variation in HIC readings, and the variation explained is statistically significant at the 0.05 level. When controlling for the child restraint, vehicle make and model explains 64 percent of the variation in chest acceleration and 63 percent of the variation in HIC.

- While the vehicle type (passenger car, SUV, LTV) had little correlation with test results, vehicle crush characteristics, such as peak acceleration, pulse duration, and amount of crush are shown to have some influence the dummies chest acceleration.

FIGURES

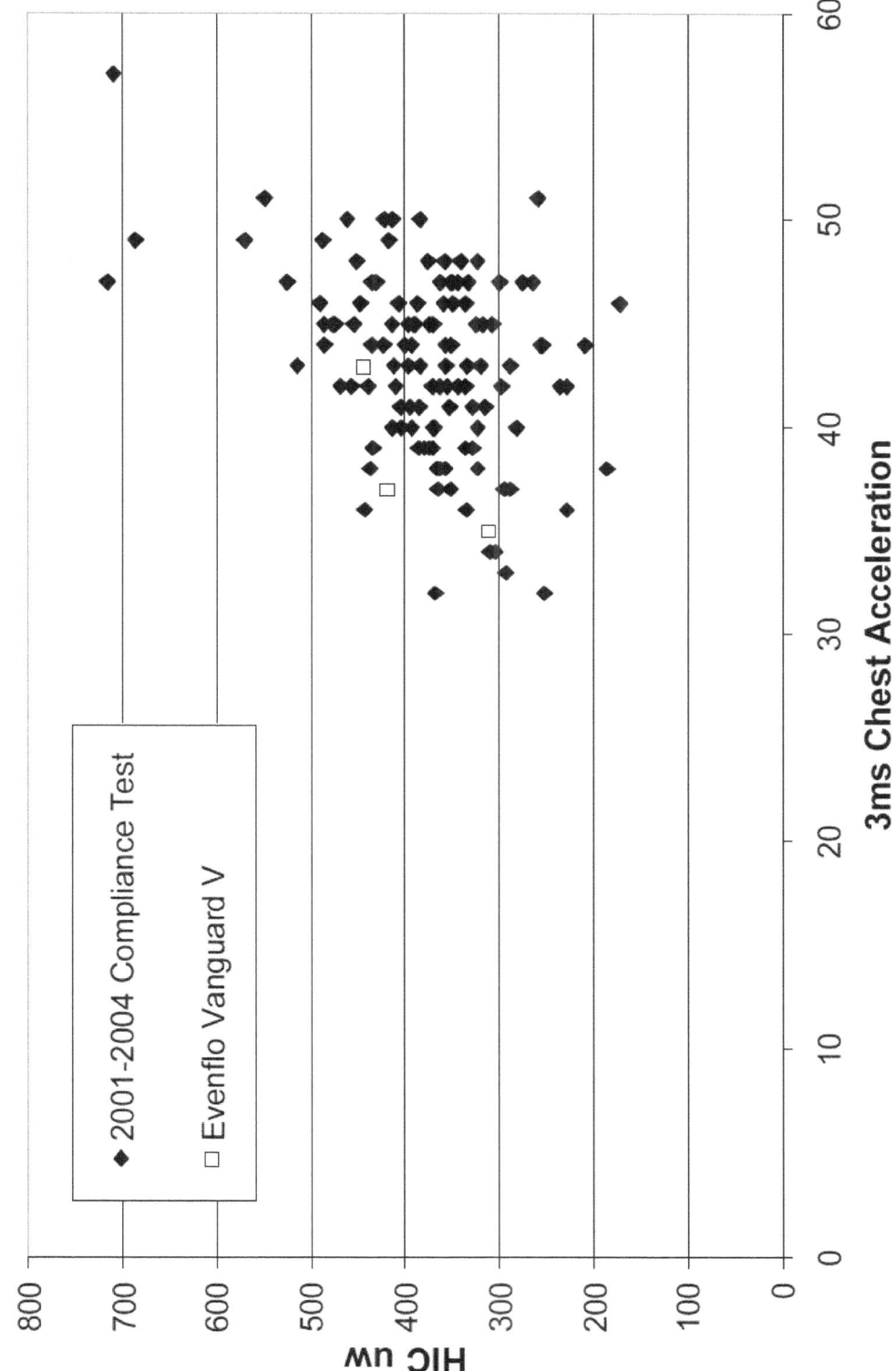

Figure 1: Evenflo Vanguard V Compliance Test

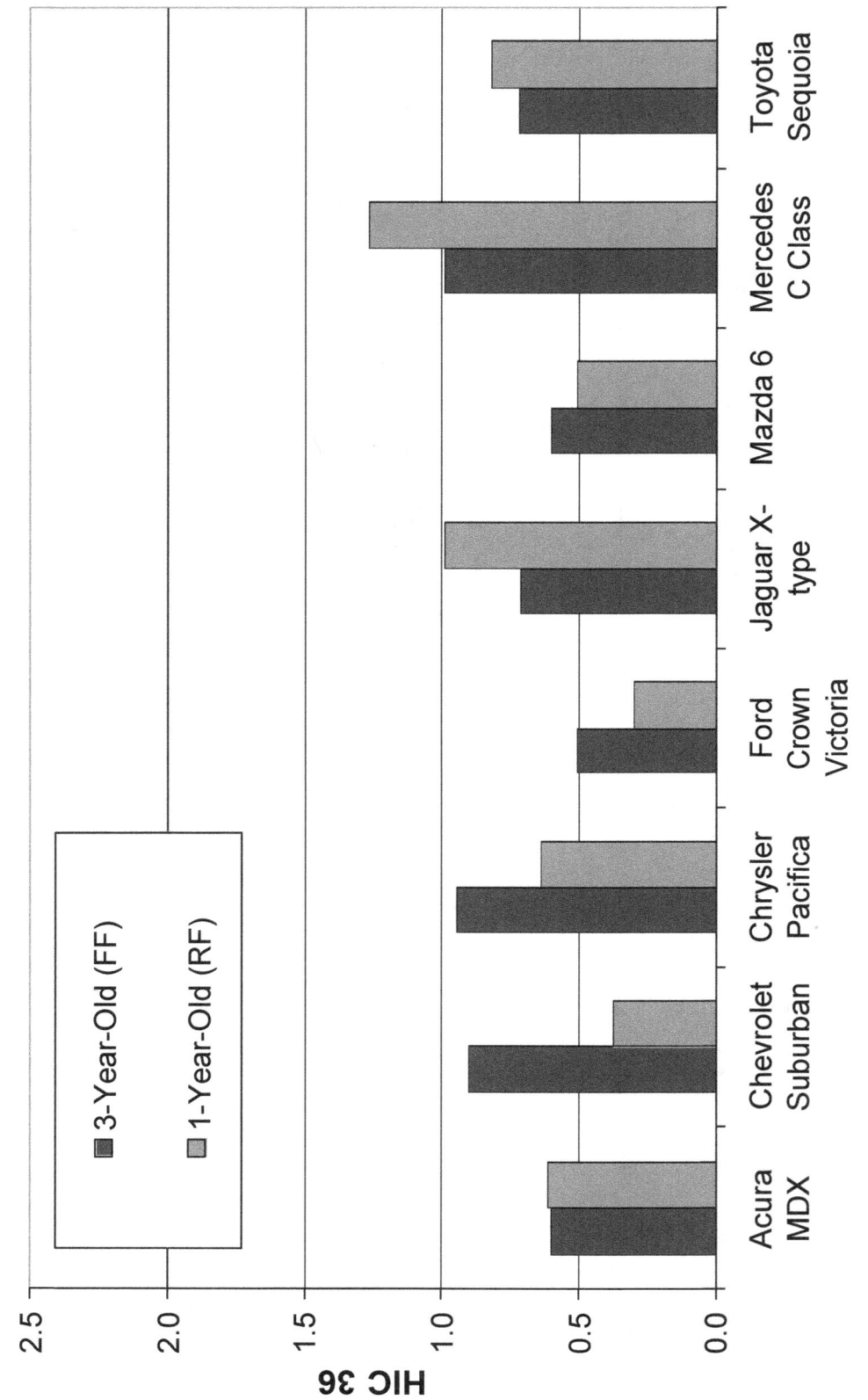

Figure 2: Normalized HIC Values for Paired Tests

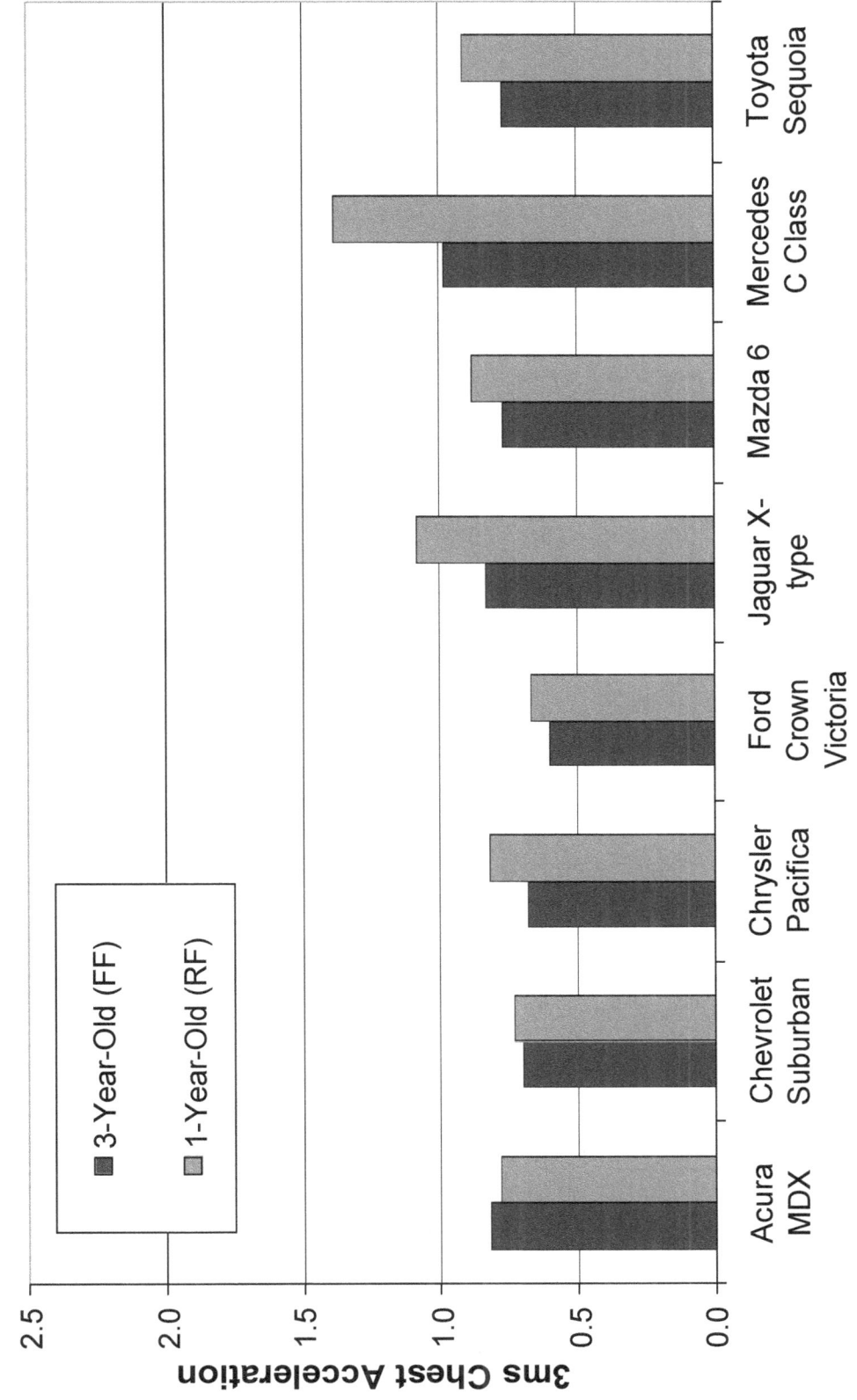

Figure 3: Normalized Chest G Values for Paired Tests

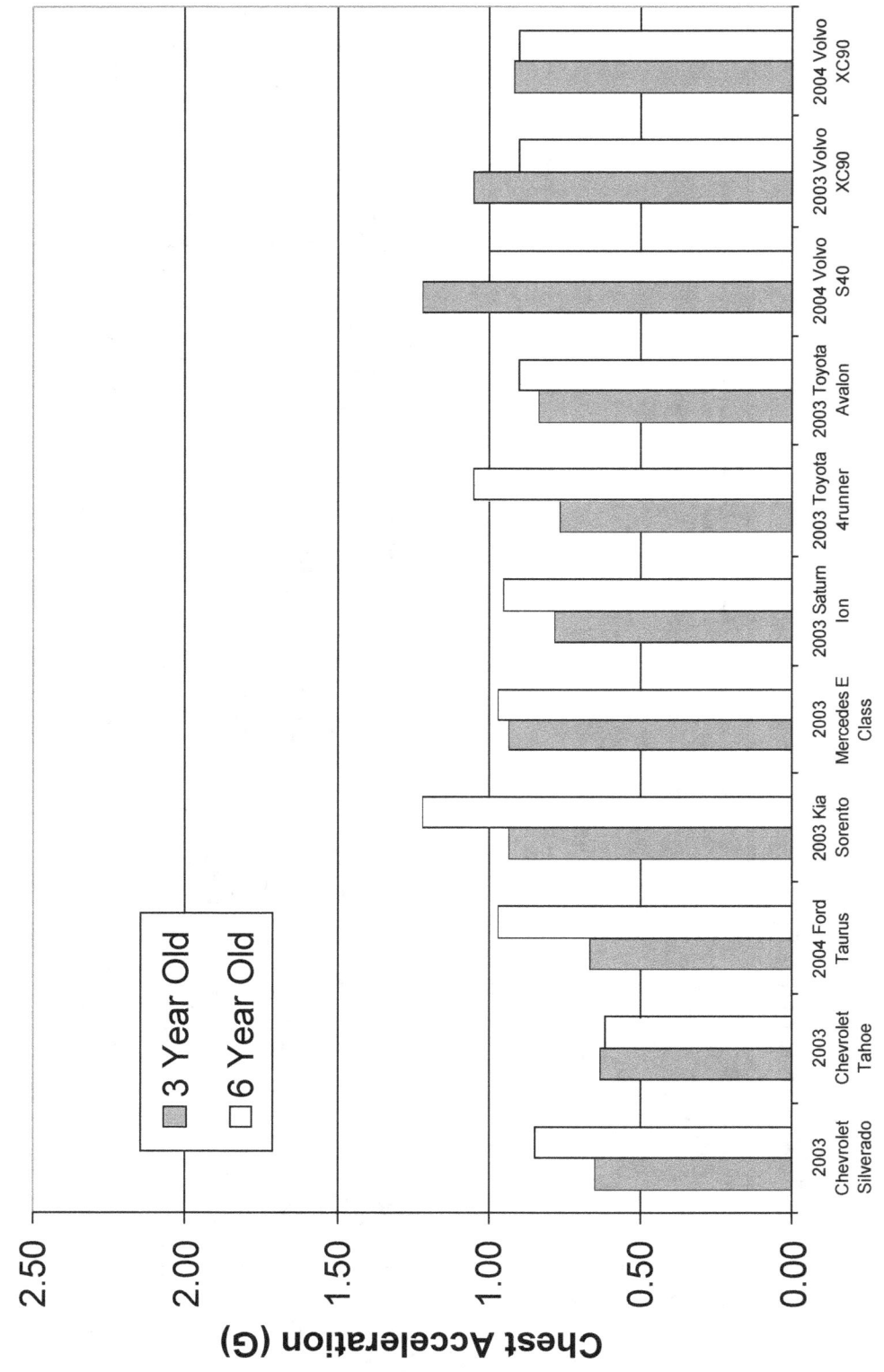

Figure 4: Normalized Chest G Values for Paired Tests

Page 18

Three-Year-Old vs Six-Year-Old

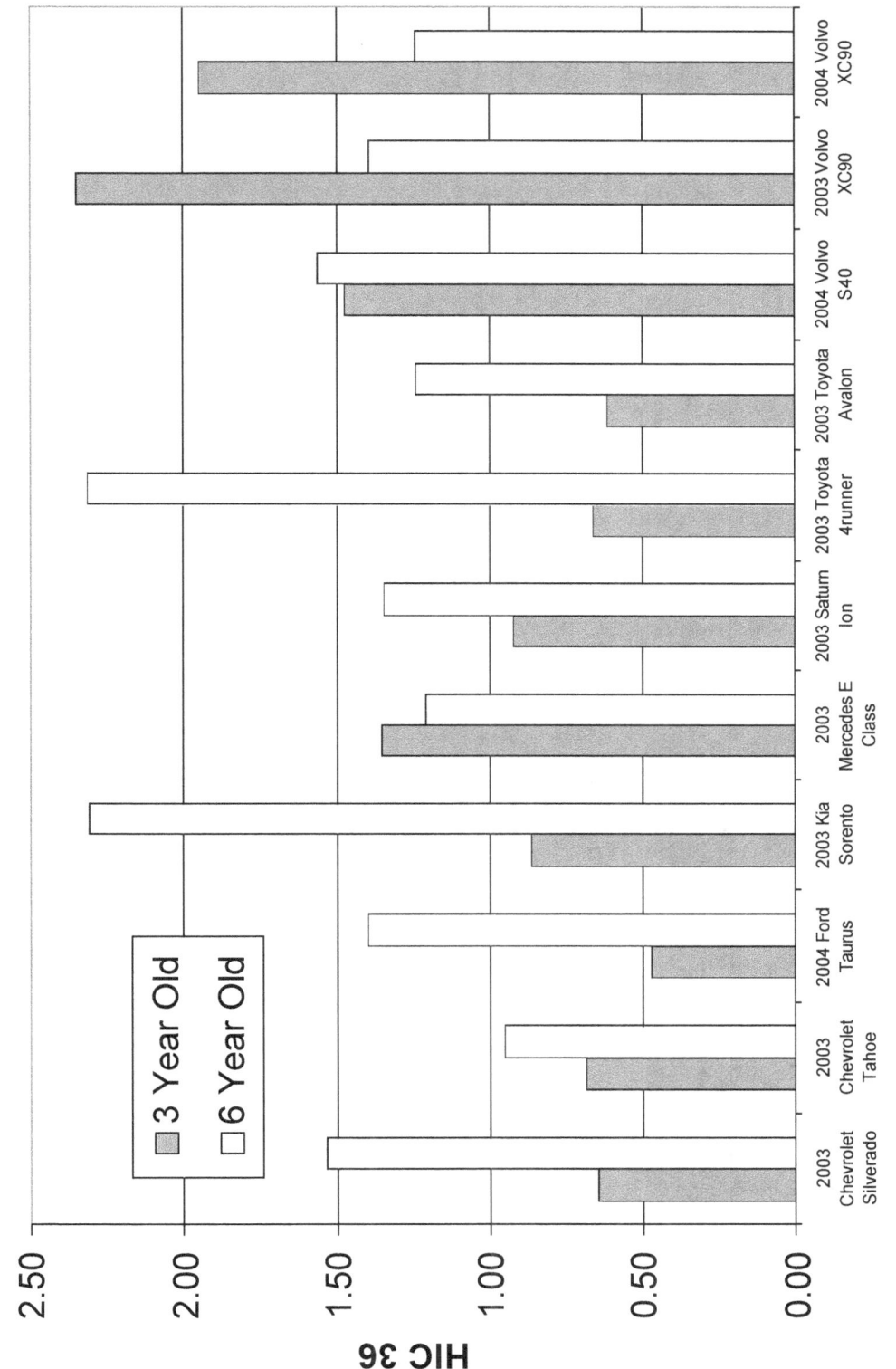

Figure 5: Normalized HIC Values for Paired Comparison

One-Year-Old Test Results

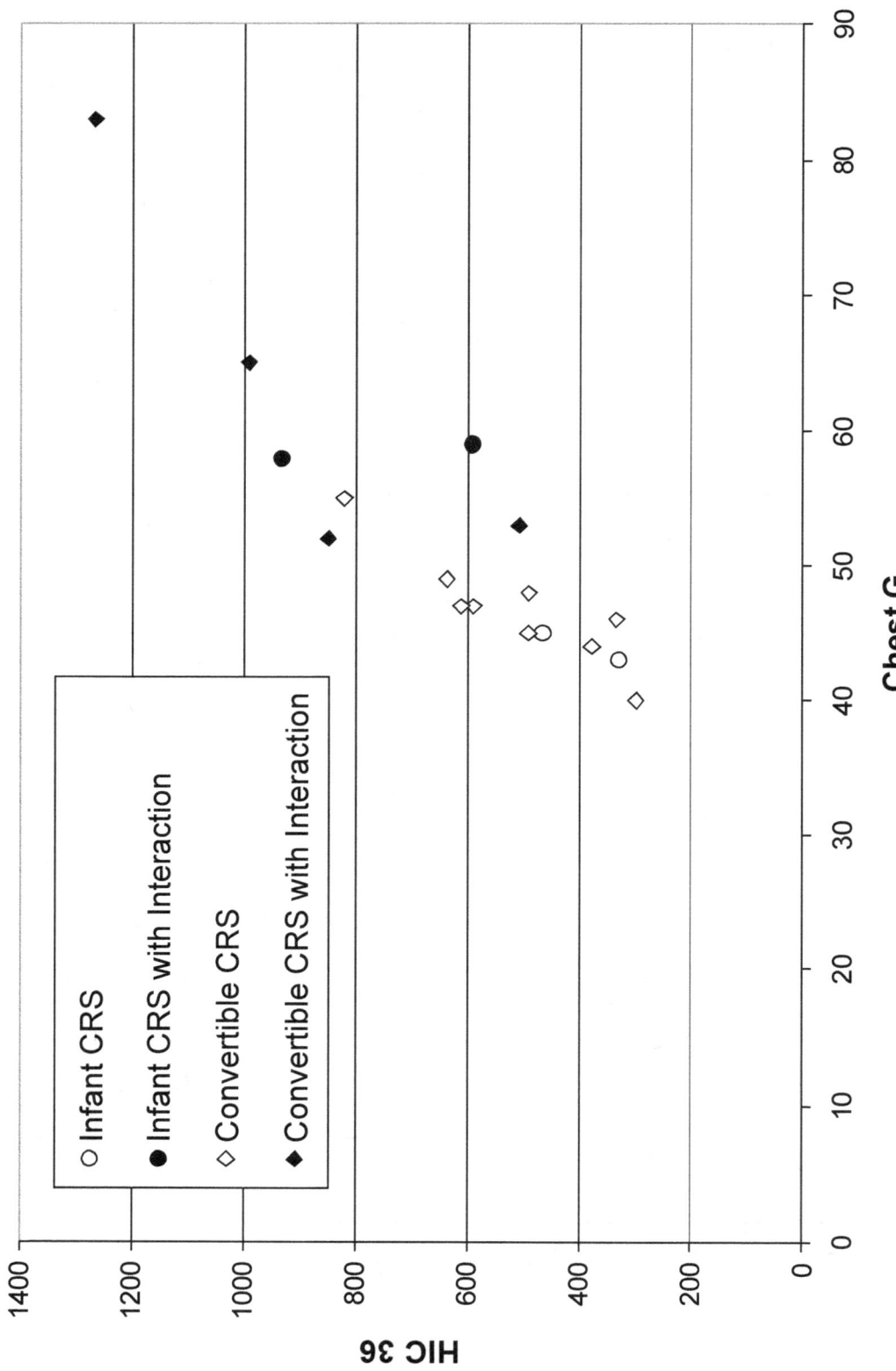

Figure 6: Results for Rear-Facing Infant and Rear-Facing Convertible Restraints

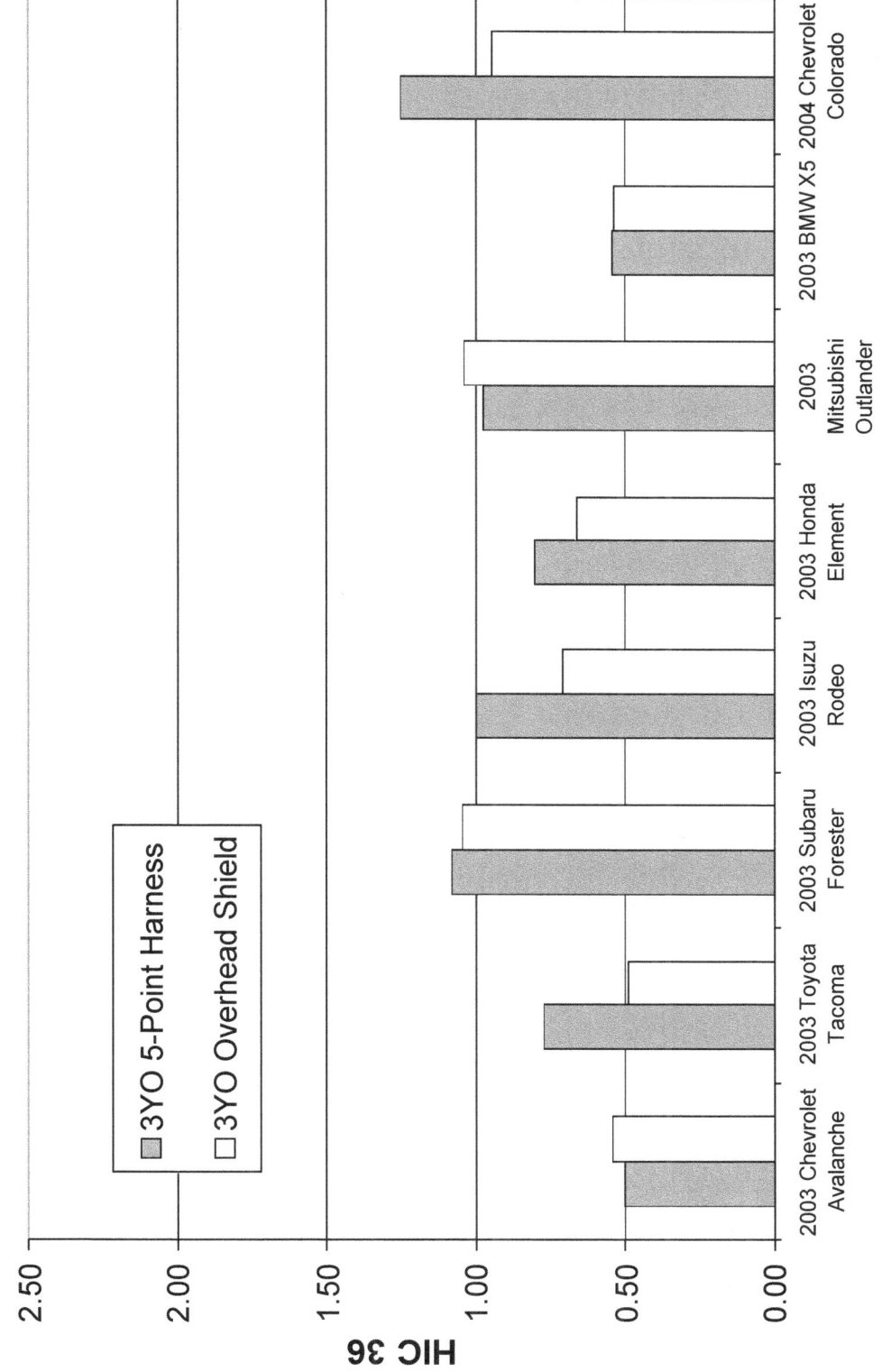

Figure 7: Normalized HIC Values for Paired Tests

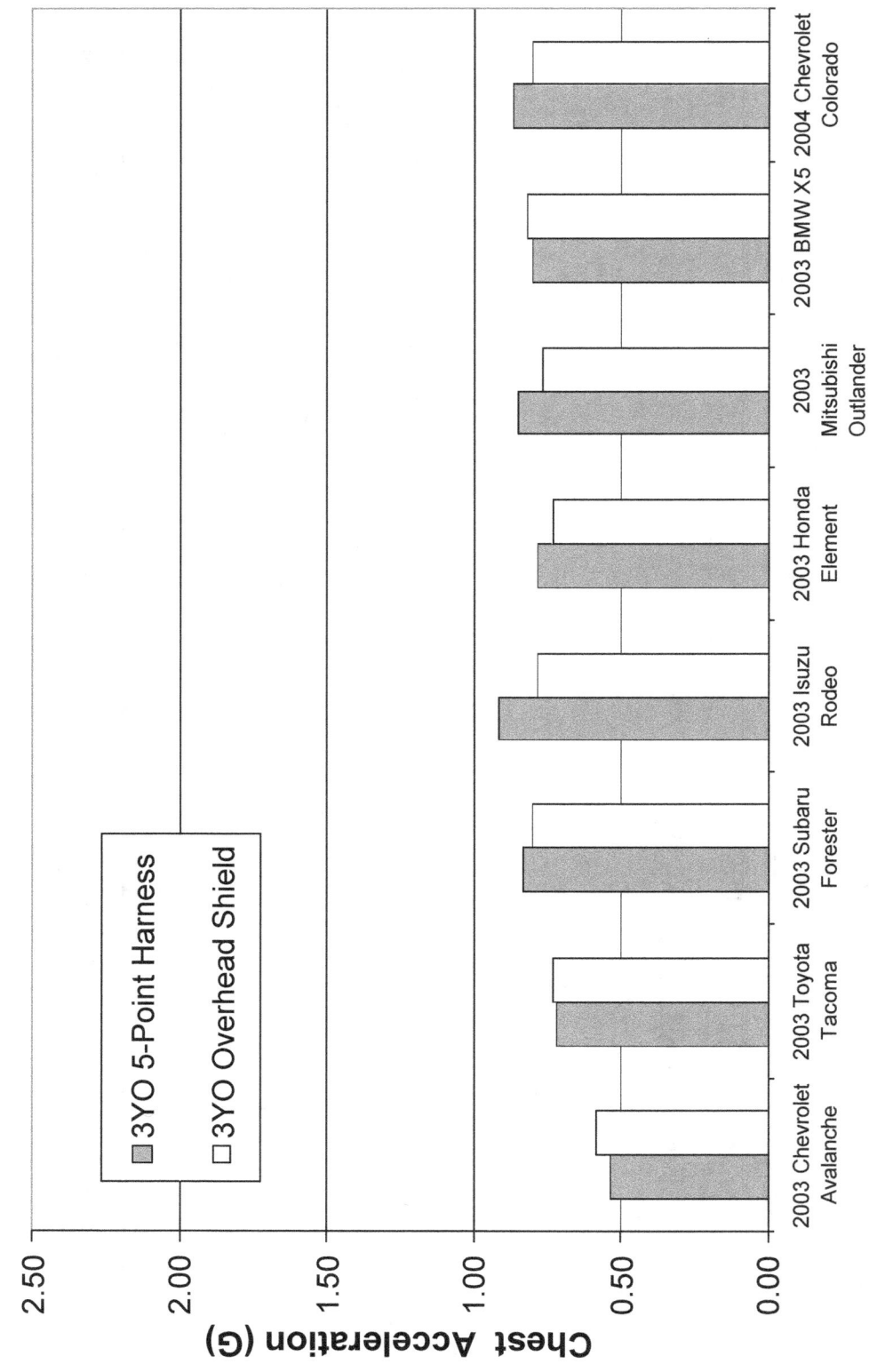

Figure 8: Normalized Chest G Values for Paired Tests

Different Brand Comparison

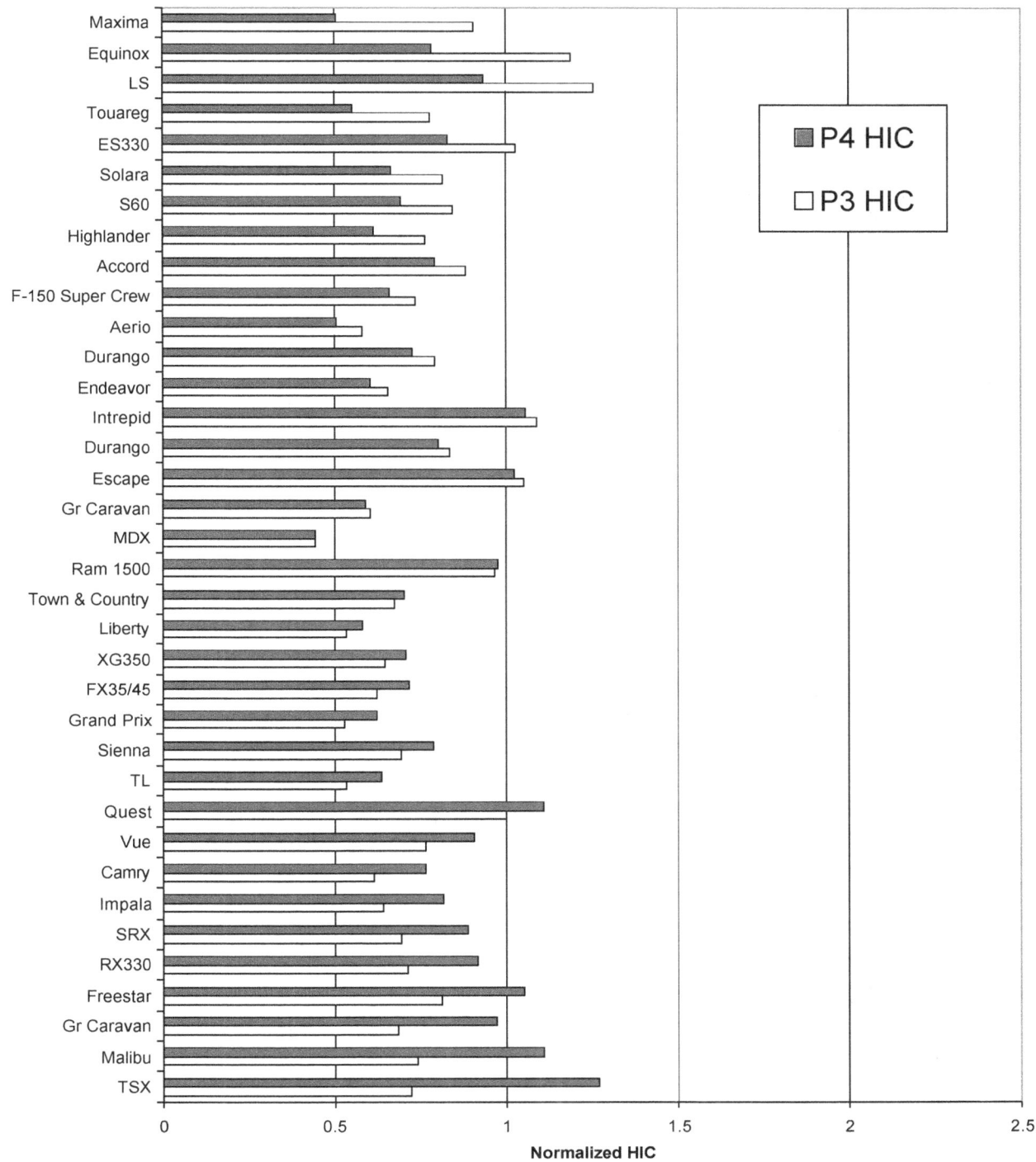

Figure 9: Normalized HIC Values for Paired Comparison

Different Brand Comparison

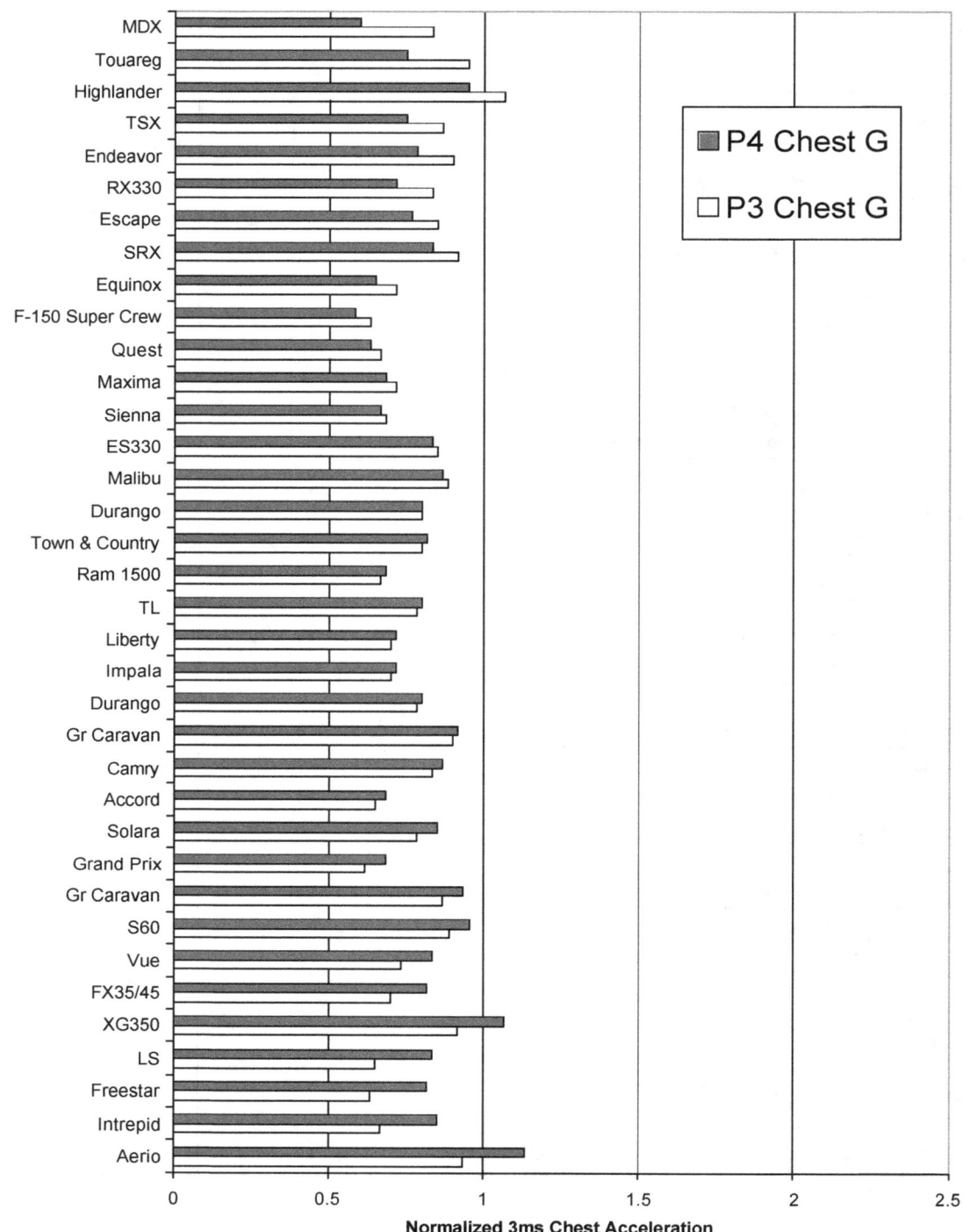

Figure 10: Normalized Chest G Values for Paired Tests

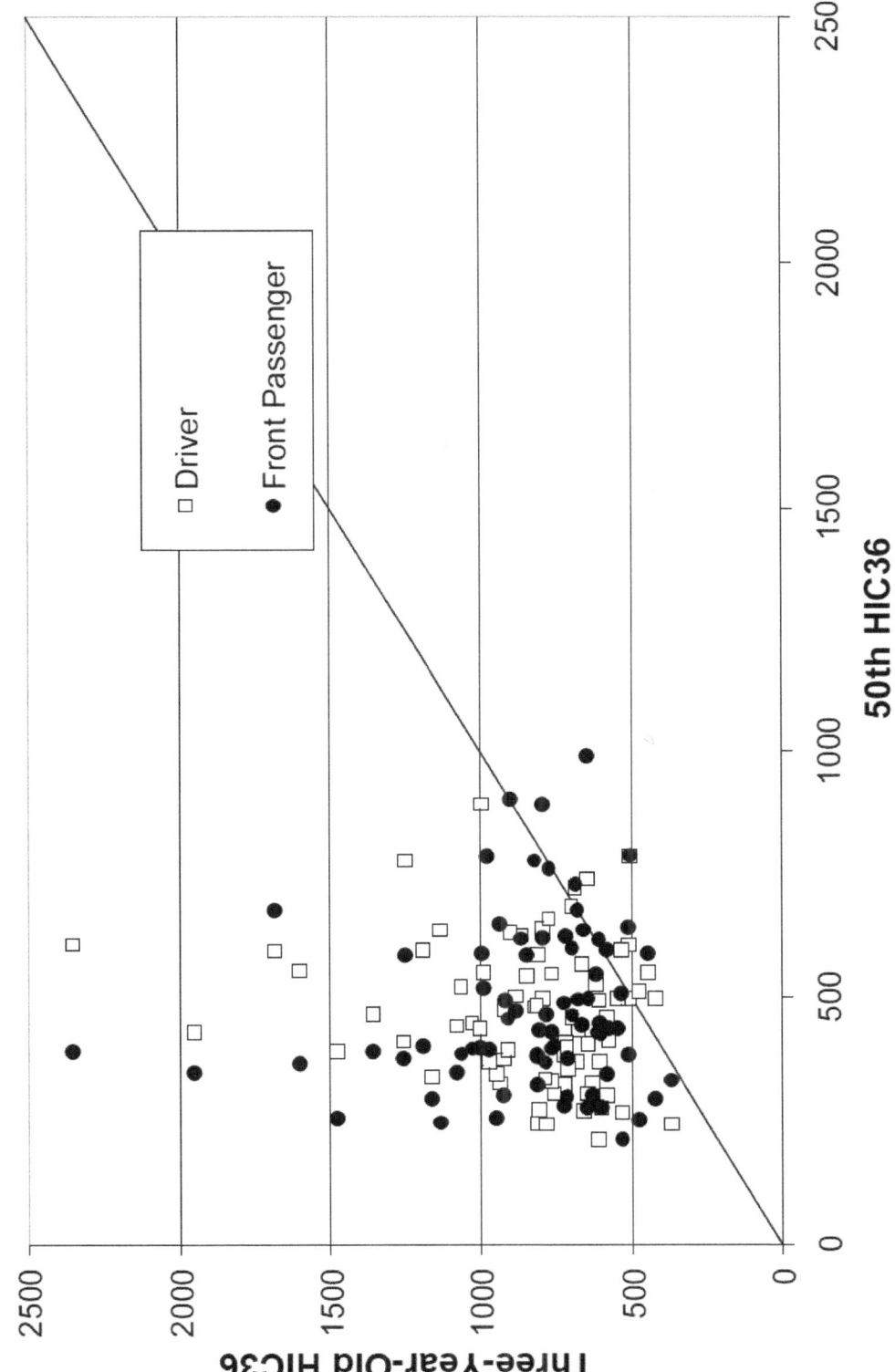

Figure 11: HIC Comparison Between Three-Year-Old and 50th-percentile

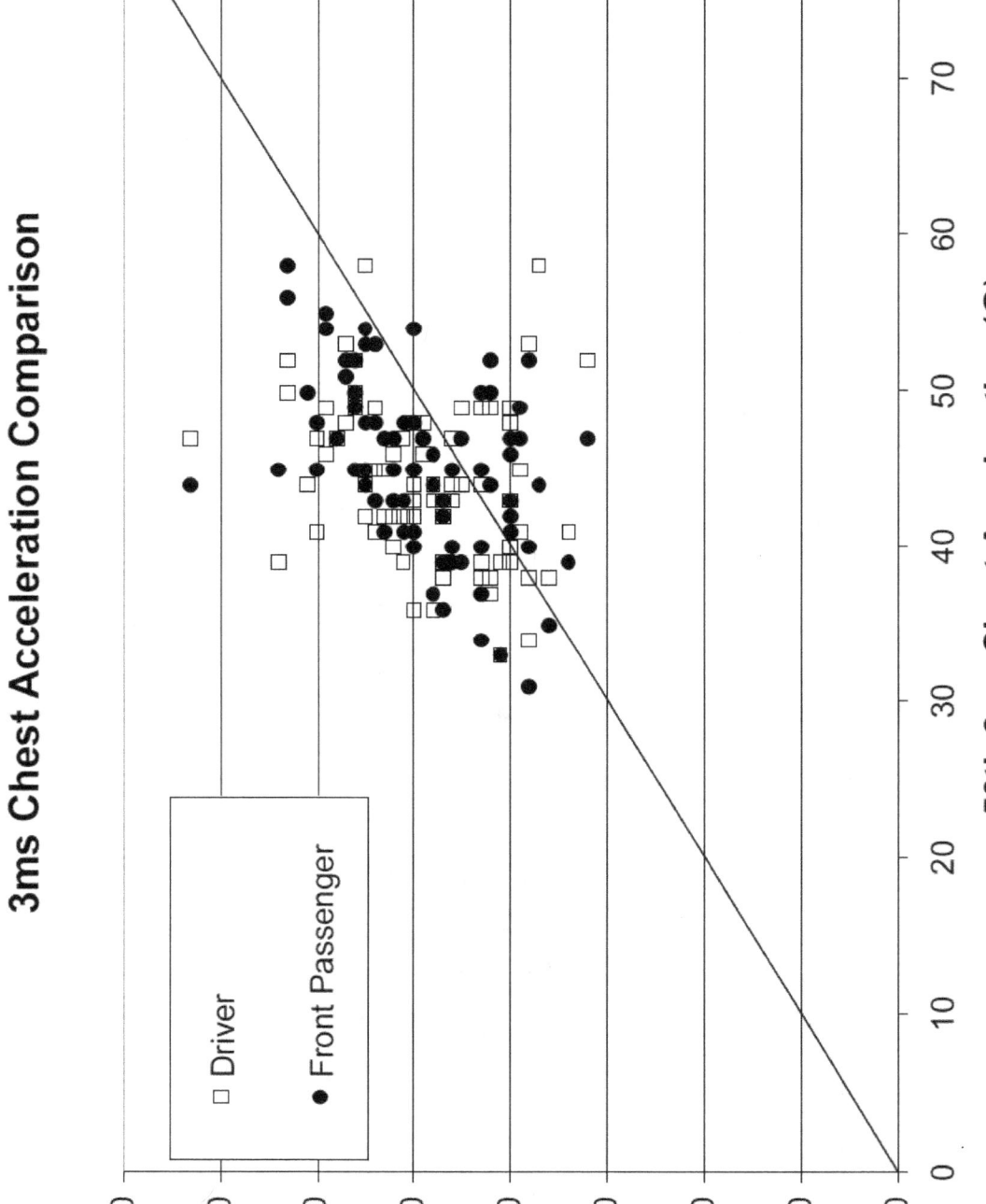

Figure 12: Chest G Comparison Between Three-Year-Old and 50th-percentile

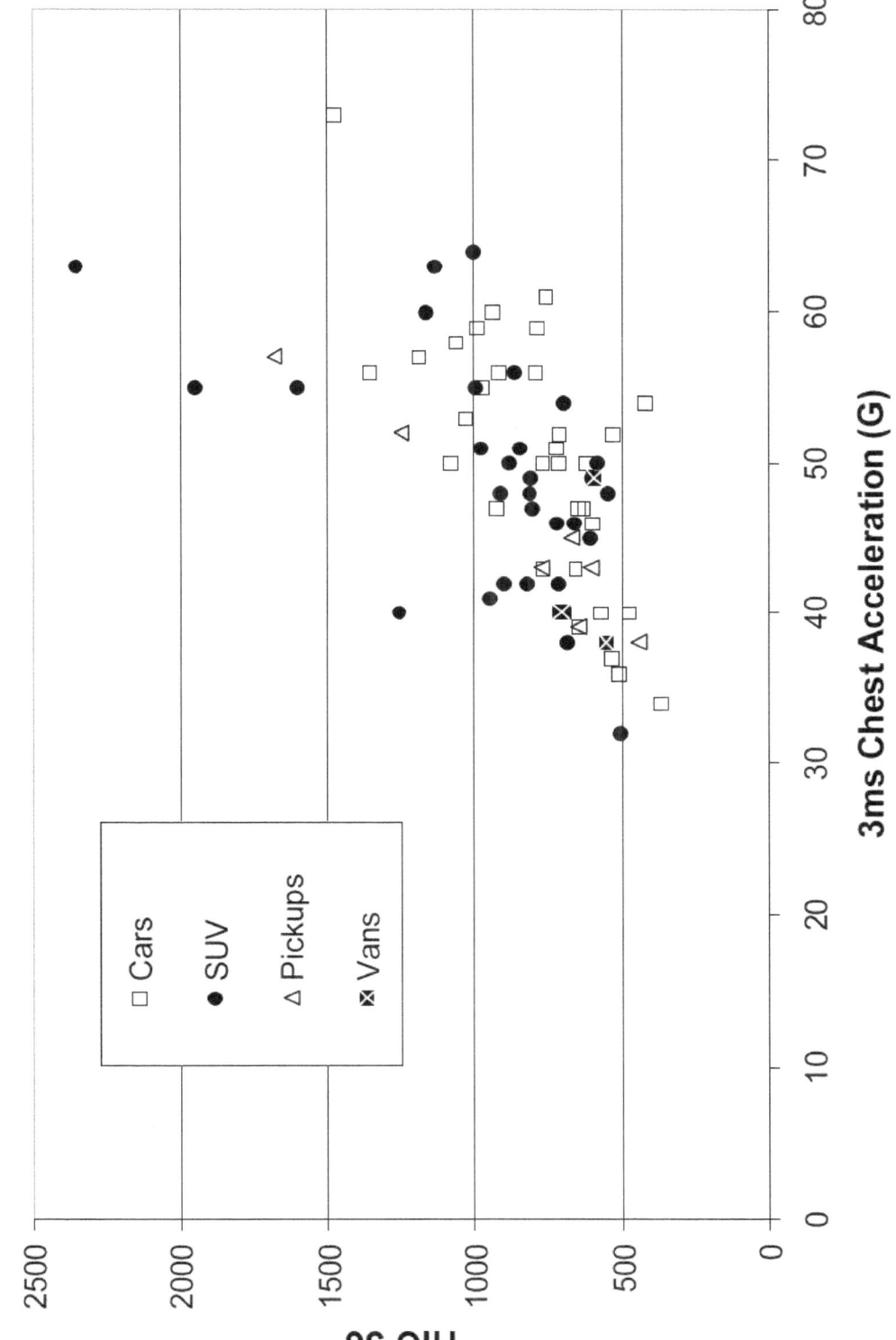

Figure 13: Three-Year-Old Injury Data Plotted by Vehicle Type

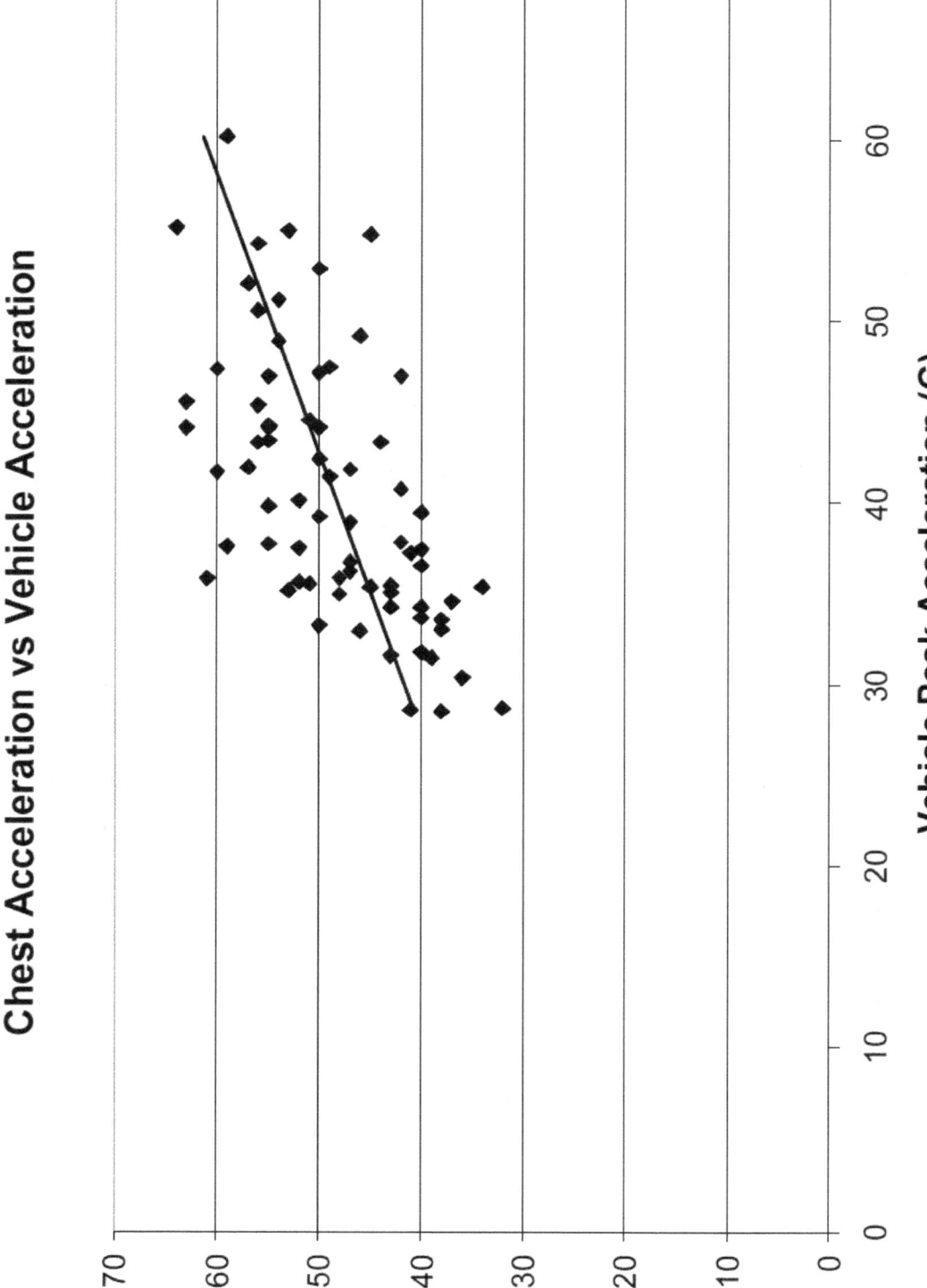

Figure 14: Chest G vs. Crash Pulse Peak Acceleration

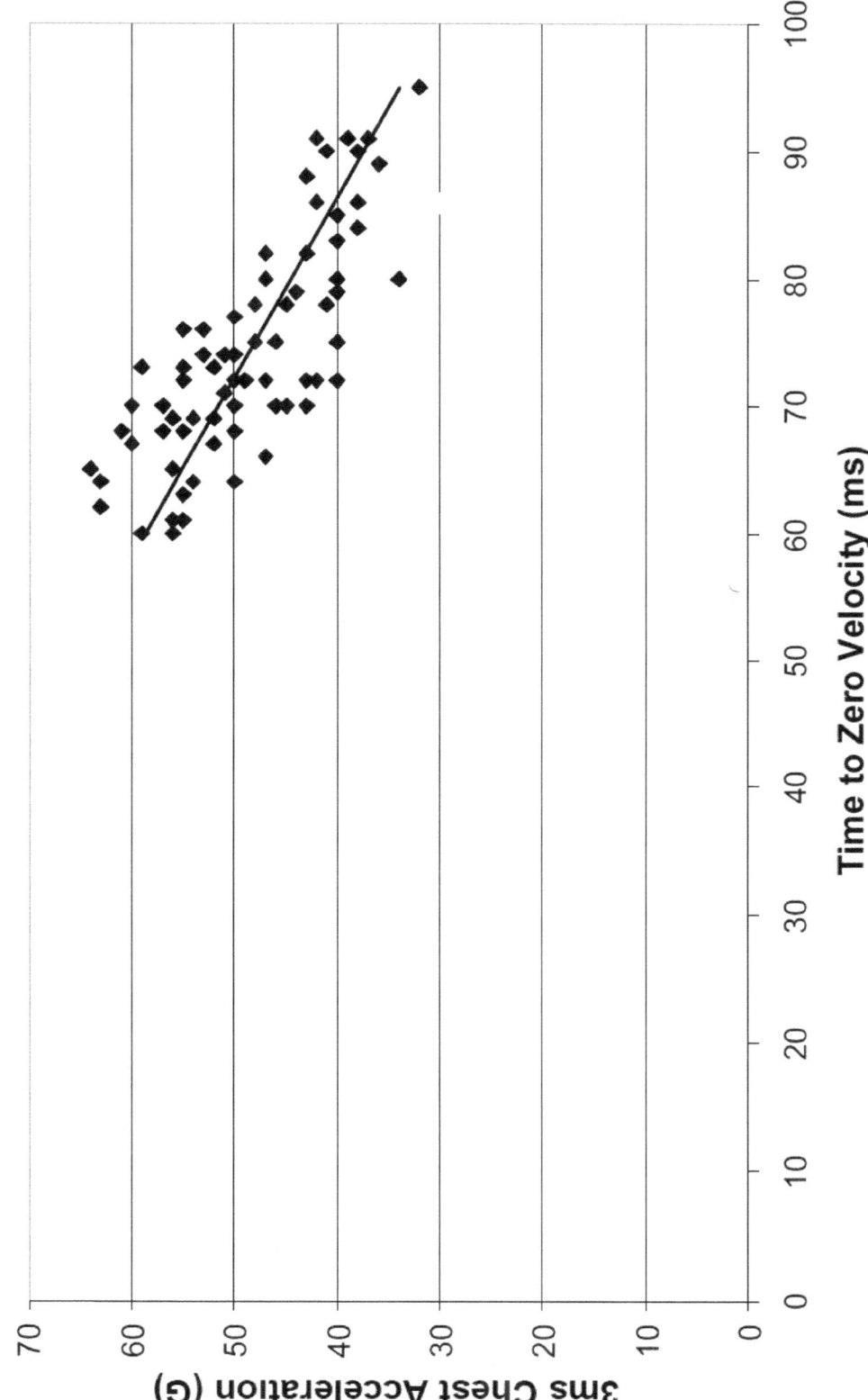

Figure 15: Chest G vs. Vehicle Crash Pulse Duration

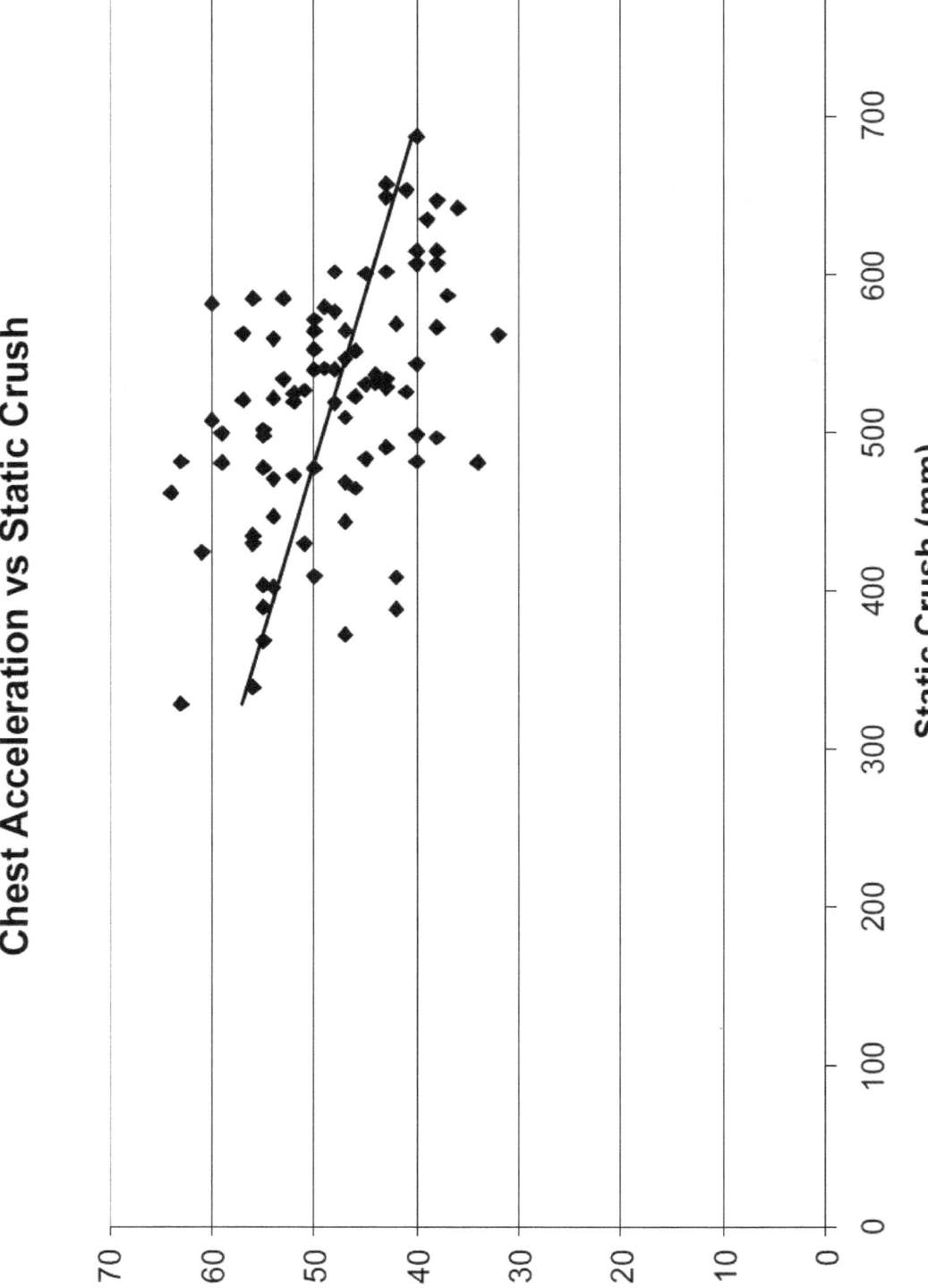

Figure 16: Chest G vs. Static Crush Measurement

APPENDIX

Appendix A

Table 1: Child Dummy Specifications

Dummy	CRABI 1YO	Hybrid III 3YO	Hybrid III 6YO
Weight (lbs)	22.0	34.1	51.6
Stature (in)	29.4	37.2	45.0

Table 2: 2001 CRS Test Matrix

Vehicle Size	Model	Left Rear	Right Rear
Light	Sentra	No CRS	Triad-LAT
	Sentra	No CRS	Emb II-LAT
	Civic 4 dr	No CRS	Horizon V-NOLAT
Compact	Echo	No CRS	Triad-LAT*
	Echo	No CRS	Hoizon V-LAT
	Elantra	No CRS	Emb II-LAT
Medium	Stratus 4dr	Triad-LAT	Triad-LAT
	Volvo S60	STE	Horizon V
	Maxima	Horizon V-NOLAT	Horizon V-LAT
	Accord	HoizonV-LAT**	Emb II-LAT
	Impala	STE	Roundabout
Heavy	Lincoln LS	Triad-NOLAT*	Triad-LAT
SUV	Escape	Emb II-NOLAT	Emb II-LAT
	Escape	Triad-NOLAT	Triad-LAT
	Durango	STE	Horizon V
	Suburban	Emb II-NOLAT	Roundabout-NOLAT
Minivan	Grand Caravan	STE	Horizon V-LAT
	Grand Caravan	Emb II-LAT	Horizon V-LAT
	Windstar	Emb II-NOLAT	Emb II-LAT
	Windstar	Triad-NOLAT	Triad-LAT

Note:

Triad-LAT	Cosco Triad with LATCH configuration
Emb II-LAT	Safe Embrace II with LATCH configuration
Triad-NOLAT	Cosco Triad with no LATCH setup
Emb II-NOLAT	Safe Embrace II with no LATCH setup
Horizon V-LAT	Evenflo Horizon V with LATCH
Roundabout-NOLAT	Britax Roundabout with no LATCH
Horizon V	Evenflo Horizon V with no LATCH configuration
STE	Century 1000 STE with no LATCH
No CRS	No child seat
*	Test Anomaly – Data not used

Table 3: 2002 CRS Test Matrix

Class	Make	Model	Type	Left rear seat	Right rear seat
Compact	Ford	Focus	4dr	No CRS	3YO in CRSA in FF
Medium	Nissan	Altima	4dr	No CRS	CRABI w/ CRS B in RF*
Medium	Subaru	Legacy	4dr	CRABI w/ CRS D in RF	CRABI w/ CRS A in RF
Medium	Toyota	Camry	4dr	CRABI w/ CRS E in RF	CRABI w/ CRS D in RF
Heavy	Cadillac	DeVille	4dr	CRABI w/ CRS D in RF	CRABI w/ CRS A in RF
PU	Dodge	Ram 1500 4x2	4dr PU	3YO w/ CRS A in FF (no LAT)	CRABI w/ CRS A in RF (no LAT)
SUV	Isuzu	Rodeo 4x4	4dr Utility	CRABI w/ CRS D in RF	CRABI w/ CRS A in RF
SUV	Chevrolet	Trai blazer 4x4	4dr Utility	CRABI w/ CRS E in RF	CRABI w/ CRS A in RF
Van	Chrysler	PT Cruiser	Van	No CRS	CRABI w/ CRS B in RF*
Van	Honda	Odyssey	Van	CRABI in CRS D in RF	CRABI w/ CRS A in RF
PU	Dodge	Dakota	PU	3YO w/ CRS A	6YO w/ CRS F

Note:
CRS A: Cosco Triad or Safety First Forerunner with LATCH
CRS B: Evenflo On-My-Way Rear Facing Child Seat
CRS C: Cosco Triad or Safety First Forerunner with Non-LATCH CRS
CRS D: GRACO SnugRide with LATCH
CRS E: GRACO SnugRide
CRS F: Century Brev erra Classic
CRABI: CRABI 12-month-old child dummy
3YO: H-III 3-year-old child dummy
6YO: H-III 6-year-old child dummy
*: Test Anomaly – Data Not Used

Table 4: 2003 CRS Test Matrix

Make	Model	BodyStyle	Rt Rear	Lt Rear	P6
Volvo	XC 90	4dr Utility	Van 5	Graco Highback	built-in
Ford	Expedition	4-dr Utility	1500STE	Accel	
Ford	ZX2	2dr	1500STE	Accel	
Nissan	Frontier	4dr PU	Van 5	Graco Comb	
Toyota	Tundra	4dr PU	Van 5	Graco Comb	
Chevrolet	Silverado 1500 4x2	PU ExCab	Van 5	Graco Highback	
Chevrolet	Tahoe 4x4	4-dr Utility	Van 5	Graco Highback	
Honda	Odyssey	Van	Van 5*	Graco Highback	
Kia	Sorento	4-dr Utility	Van 5	Graco Highback	
Mercedes	E Class	4dr	Van 5	Graco Highback	
Saturn	Ion	4-dr	Van 5	Graco Highback	
Toyota	4-Runner	4dr Utility	Van 5	Graco Highback	
Toyota	Avalon	4-dr	Van 5	Graco Highback	
Acura	MDX	4dr Utility	Van 5	RF of Van 5	
Chevrolet	Suburban 1500 4x4	4-dr Utility	Van 5	RF of Van 5	
Chrysler	Pacifica (option)	4-dr Utility	Van 5	RF of Van 5	
Ford	Crown Victoria	4-dr	Van 5	RF of Van 5	
Honda	Accord 4dr	4-dr	Van 5	RF of Van 5	
Jaguar	X-Type	4dr	Van 5	RF of Van 5	
Mazda	Mazda 6	4-dr	Van 5	RF of Van 5	
Mercedes	C Class	4dr	Van 5	RF of Van 5	
Toyota	Sequoia	4dr Utility	Van 5	RF of Van 5	
Chevrolet	Avalanche 1500 4x4	4dr Utility	Van 5	Titan (Comfort)	
Toyota	Tacoma 4dr	4dr PU	Van 5	Titan (Comfort)	
BMW	X5	4dr Utility	Van 5	Van Comfort	
Honda	Element	4dr Utility	Van 5	Van Comfort	
Isuzu	Rodeo	4-dr Utility	Van 5	Van Comfort	
Mitsubishi	Outlander	4dr Utility	Van 5	Van Comfort	
Nissan	Murano	4dr Utility	Van 5*	Van Comfort	
Subaru	Forester	4w	Van 5	Van Comfort	
Chevrolet	Cavalier	2-dr	1500STE	XX	
Honda	Accord	2-dr	1500STE	XX	
Hyundai	Accent	4-dr	Van 5	XX	

XX is no CRS used
Titan is same seat as Van Comfort Overhead Shield w/o LATCH
Van 5 is Evenflo Vanguard 5 point harness Convertible Seat with LATCH
Van Comfort is Vanguard 5 seat with Overhead Shield with LATCH
RF of Van 5 is Evenflo Vanguard 5 point harness Convertible Seat in rear facing mode
Graco Highback is Graco My Cargo Highback Booster seat
1500 STE is Century 1500 STE convert ble seat
Accel is Century Accel Overhead Shield Child seat
Graco Combo is Graco Combination seat with LATCH
* Test Anomaly – Data Not Used

Table 5: Comparison between Vanguard 5 and Roundabout

Model	Evenflo Vanguard 5		Britax Roundabout	
	HIC 36	Chest G	HIC 36	Chest G
Acura TL	646	47	710	48
Chevrolet Malibu	1027	53	830	52
Dodge Intrepid	694	40	791	51
Hyundai XG350	970	55	976	64
Lincoln LS	641	39	816	50
Mitsubishi Endeavor	694	54	889	47
Suzuki Aerio	793	56	729	68
Toyota Camry	765	50	906	52
Toyota Highlander	1000	64	1107	57
Toyota Sienna	676	41	705	40
Toyota Solara	625	47	716	51

Appendix B
Face-to-Chest Contact Analysis

The 2003 NCAP tests involving the Hybrid III six-year-old dummy displayed dummy kinematics with face contact to the upper torso. Data traces confirmed this contact. Typically, the face-to-chest contact happens between 100 and 115 ms. Using film analysis, the time of the contact event was compared to the time window of the HIC calculation. In half of the cases the contact occurred inside the HIC window, while in the others, it occurred outside the HIC window.

Contact inside HIC window	Contact outside HIC window
Toyota Avalon	Toyota 4Runner
Mercedes E320	Chevrolet Tahoe
Chevrolet Silverado	Honda Odyssey
Kia Sorento	Saturn Ion
Volvo XC90 (P4)	Volvo XC90 (P6)

Although the contact occurred during the HIC calculation for half of these tests, the contact does not seem to be a large contributor to the HIC values that occurred during the test. The influence of the face-to-chest contact was artificially removed from the head resultant acceleration and a new HIC was computed and compared. Figures B1 and B2 show two samples where the contact was artificially removed. The new HIC calculations are shown in Table B1.

The effects of the face-to-chest contact on chest acceleration were also investigated. The chest acceleration plots do not show much effect from the contact. In fact, the spike is only evident in the raw data and once the curve is filtered, the contact is not seen. In addition, the contact happens well after the 3ms chest G window, and therefore, face-to-chest contact has no effect on chest acceleration measurements.

Table B1: Recalculation of HIC values with face-to-chest contact removed

Make	Model	Original			Modified			Spike Time
		HIC	t1	t2	HIC	t1	t2	
Toyota	Avalon	1241.0	68.0	104.0	1198.9	67.7	103.7	100
Mercedes	E320	1210.2	62.1	98.1	1075.7	60.1	96.1	84
Chevrolet	Silverado	1532.0	71.6	107.6	1531.4	71.2	107.2	106
Kia	Sorento	2310.9	57.6	92.8	2237.2	58.2	87.2	87
Volvo	XC90	1392.7	53.0	89.0	1340.5	51.8	87.8	79

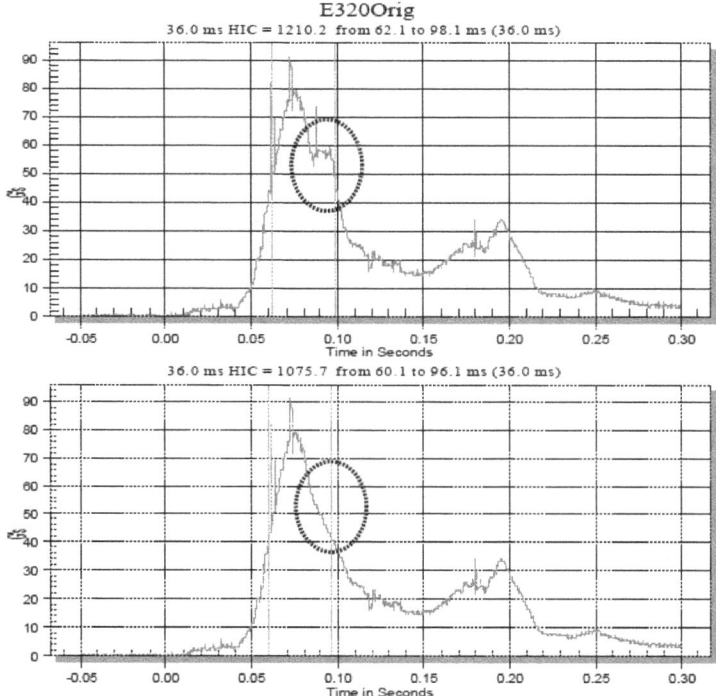

Figure B1: 2003 Mercedes E320 6YO HIC readings, with and without face-to-chest contact

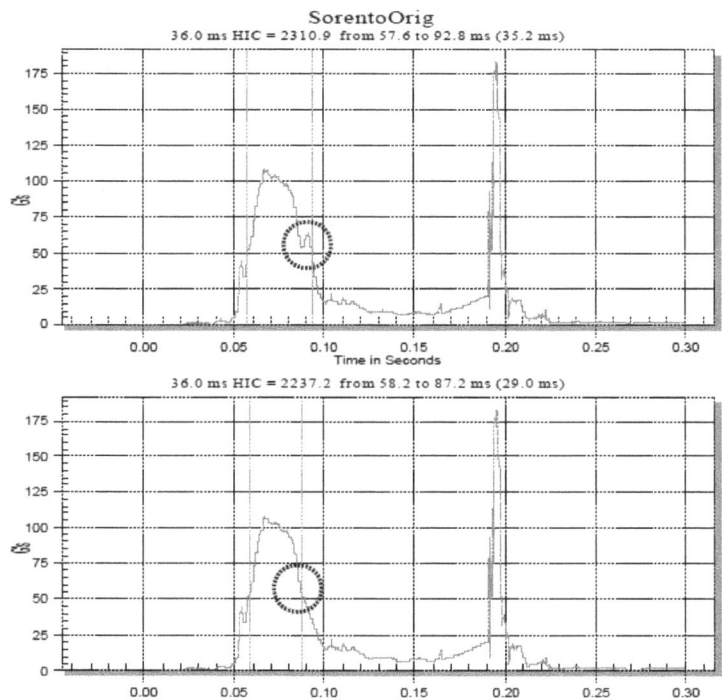

Figure B2: 2003 Kia Sorento 6YO HIC readings, with and without face-to-chest contact

Appendix C

Table 6: Child Dummy Injury Readings for 2001-2004

Test No.	Vehicle	Child Restraint	Dummy	Position	HIC15	HIC36	Chest G
3537	2001 Toyota Echo	Cosco Triad	3YO	P3	302	667	54
3548	2001 Lincoln LS	Cosco Triad	3YO	P3	394	663	47
3548	2001 Lincoln LS	Cosco Triad	3YO	P4	1029	1387	53
3549	2001 Dodge Stratus	Cosco Triad	3YO	P3	368	631	44
3549	2001 Dodge Stratus	Cosco Triad	3YO	P4	463	760	45
3553	2001 Chevrolet Suburban	Britax Roundabout	3YO	P3	564	884	38
3562	2001 Nissan Sentra	Cosco Triad	3YO	P3	342	628	43
3563	2001 Hyundai Elantra	Fisher Price Safe Embrace II	3YO	P3	450	671	48
3573	2001 Dodge Gr Caravan	Evenflo Horizon V	3YO	P3	733	1050	54
3573	2001 Dodge Gr Caravan	Century STE	3YO	P4	770	1023	55
3593	2001 Ford Escape	Fisher Price Safe Embrace II	3YO	P3	387	642	47
3593	2001 Ford Escape	Fisher Price Safe Embrace II	3YO	P4	493	780	53
3594	2001 Ford Windstar	Fisher Price Safe Embrace II	3YO	P3	371	653	38
3594	2001 Ford Windstar	Fisher Price Safe Embrace II	3YO	P4	342	606	38
4215	2002 Nissan Altima	Evenflo Cozy Carry	1YO	P3	288	288	43
4216	2002 Ford Focus	Safety 1st Forerunner	3YO	P3	460	678	45
4230	2002 Chrysler PT Cruiser	Evenflo Cozy Carry	1YO	P3	1169	1216	72
4237	2002 Nissan Frontier	none - jump seat	6YO	P3	988	992	48
4237	2002 Nissan Frontier	none - jump seat	3YO	P4	490	539	65
4238	2002 Cadillac DeVille	Safety 1st Forerunner	1YO	P3	270	589	47
4238	2002 Cadillac DeVille	Graco Snugride	1YO	P4	96	138	35
4240	2002 Dodge Ram 1500	Safety 1st Forerunner	1YO	P3	841	849	52
4240	2002 Dodge Ram 1500	Safety 1st Forerunner	3YO	P4	833	1180	54
4241	2002 Isuzu Rodeo	Safety 1st Forerunner	1YO	P3	243	333	46
4241	2002 Isuzu Rodeo	Graco Snugride	1YO	P4	187	328	43
4242	2002 Honda Odyssey	Safety 1st Forerunner	1YO	P3	178	326	43
4242	2002 Honda Odyssey	Graco Snugride	1YO	P4	209	466	45
4243	2002 Toyota Camry	Graco Snugride	1YO	P3	457	933	58
4243	2002 Toyota Camry	Graco Snugride	1YO	P4	390	728	41
4244	2002 Chevrolet Trailblazer	Safety 1st Forerunner	1YO	P3	312	491	45
4244	2002 Chevrolet Trailblazer	Graco Snugride	1YO	P4	356	708	*
4251	2002 Subaru Legacy	Safety 1st Forerunner	1YO	P3	283	490	48

Appendix C

Test No.	Vehicle	Child Restraint	Dummy	Position	HIC15	HIC36	Chest G
4251	2002 Subaru Legacy	Graco Snugride	1YO	P4	522	592	59
4252	2002 Dodge Dakota	Breverra Classic	6YO	P3	477	930	56
4252	2002 Dodge Dakota	Safety 1st Forerunner	3YO	P4	1665	1880	59
4435	2003 Ford Expedition	Century 1500 STE	3YO	P3	354	581	43
4435	2003 Ford Expedition	Century Accel Overhead	3YO	P4	460	757	51
4445	2003 Chevrolet Cavalier	Century 1500 STE	3YO	P3	344	508	55
4446	2003 Ford ZX2	Century 1500 STE	3YO	P3	505	792	54
4446	2003 Ford ZX2	Century Accel Overhead	3YO	P4	390	645	38
4457	2003 Honda Accord 2dr	Century 1500 STE	3YO	P3	520	808	53
4459	2003 Toyota Tundra	Evenflo Vanguard V	3YO	P3	383	673	45
4459	2003 Toyota Tundra	Graco Platinum CarGo	3YO	P4	337	604	48
4460	2003 Nissan Frontier	Evenflo Vanguard V	3YO	P3	1619	1680	57
4460	2003 Nissan Frontier	Graco Platinum CarGo	3YO	P4	1112	1231	63
4463	2003 Honda Odyssey	Evenflo Vanguard V	3YO	P3	772	772	*
4463	2003 Honda Odyssey	Graco My CarGo	6YO	P4	594	1048	39
4464	2003 Chevrolet Avalanche	Evenflo Vanguard V	3YO	P3	245	502	32
4464	2003 Chevrolet Avalanche	Evenflo Titan OS	3YO	P4	258	542	35
4472	2003 Chevrolet Silverado	Evenflo Vanguard V	3YO	P3	333	645	39
4472	2003 Chevrolet Silverado	Graco My CarGo	6YO	P4	813	1532	51
4473	2003 Hyundai Accent	Evenflo Vanguard V	3YO	P3	685	935	60
4476	2003 Ford Crown Victoria	Evenflo Vanguard V	3YO	P3	281	507	36
4476	2003 Ford Crown Victoria	Evenflo Vanguard V	1YO	P4	190	298	40
4478	2003 Toyota Tacoma	Evenflo Vanguard V	3YO	P3	482	771	43
4478	2003 Toyota Tacoma	Evenflo Titan OS	3YO	P4	281	490	44
4479	2003 Subaru Forester	Evenflo Vanguard V	3YO	P3	663	1078	50
4479	2003 Subaru Forester	Evenflo Vanguard Comfort	3YO	P4	668	1042	48
4483	2003 Mercedes E Class	Evenflo Vanguard V	3YO	P3	860	1355	56
4483	2003 Mercedes E Class	Graco My CarGo	6YO	P4	724	1208	58
4484	2003 Jaguar X-type	Evenflo Vanguard V	3YO	P3	561	714	50
4484	2003 Jaguar X-type	Evenflo Vanguard V	1YO	P4	507	991	65
4485	2003 Honda Accord 4dr	Evenflo Vanguard V	3YO	P3	290	366	34
4485	2003 Honda Accord 4dr	Evenflo Vanguard V	1YO	P4	*	*	64
4486	2003 Toyota Avalon	Evenflo Vanguard V	3YO	P3	340	614	50
4486	2003 Toyota Avalon	Graco My CarGo	6YO	P4	887	1241	54

Appendix C

Test No.	Vehicle	Child Restraint	Dummy	Position	HIC15	HIC36	Chest G
4487	2003 Saturn Ion	Evenflo Vanguard V	3YO	P3	514	921	47
4487	2003 Saturn Ion	Graco My CarGo	6YO	P4	927	1346	57
4488	2003 Mazda 6	Evenflo Vanguard V	3YO	P3	318	598	46
4488	2003 Mazda 6	Evenflo Vanguard V	1YO	P4	507	507	53
4491	2003 Mercedes C Class	Evenflo Vanguard V	3YO	P3	753	990	59
4491	2003 Mercedes C Class	Evenflo Vanguard V	1YO	P4	731	1266	83
4493	2003 Volvo XC90	Evenflo Vanguard V	3YO	P3	1624	2351	63
4493	2003 Volvo XC90	Graco My Cargo	6YO	P4	854	1393	54
4500	2003 Isuzu Rodeo	Evenflo Vanguard V	3YO	P3	560	995	55
4500	2003 Isuzu Rodeo	Evenflo Vanguard Comfort	3YO	P4	341	709	47
4544	2003 Nissan Murano	Evenflo Vanguard V	3YO	P3	875	1598	55
4544	2003 Nissan Murano	Evenflo Vanguard Comfort	3YO	P4	686	1488	46
4545	2003 Toyota Sequoia	Evenflo Vanguard V	3YO	P3	390	719	46
4545	2003 Toyota Sequoia	Evenflo Vanguard V	1YO	P4	499	820	55
4546	2003 Toyota 4runner	Evenflo Vanguard V	3YO	P3	371	660	46
4546	2003 Toyota 4runner	Graco My CarGo	6YO	P4	1763	2313	63
4548	2003 Kia Sorento	Evenflo Vanguard V	3YO	P3	574	862	56
4548	2003 Kia Sorento	Graco My CarGo	6YO	P4	1564	2311	73
4549	2003 Chevrolet Tahoe	Evenflo Vanguard V	3YO	P3	335	683	38
4549	2003 Chevrolet Tahoe	Graco My CarGo	6YO	P4	623	951	37
4553	2003 Acura MDX	Evenflo Vanguard V	3YO	P3	463	599	49
4553	2003 Acura MDX	Evenflo Vanguard V	1YO	P4	318	611	47
4555	2003 Honda Element	Evenflo Vanguard V	3YO	P3	584	803	47
4555	2003 Honda Element	Evenflo Vanguard Comfort	3YO	P4	389	663	44
4559	2003 Mitsubishi Outlander	Evenflo Vanguard V	3YO	P3	643	976	51
4559	2003 Mitsubishi Outlander	Evenflo Vanguard Comfort	3YO	P4	538	1038	46
4560	2003 BMW X5	Evenflo Vanguard V	3YO	P3	341	543	48
4560	2003 BMW X5	Evenflo Vanguard Comfort	3YO	P4	383	537	49
4567	2003 Chevrolet Suburban	Evenflo Vanguard V	3YO	P3	492	900	42
4567	2003 Chevrolet Suburban	Evenflo Vanguard V	1YO	P4	179	377	44
4572	2004 Chrysler Pacifica	Evenflo Vanguard V	3YO	P3	474	946	41
4572	2004 Chrysler Pacifica	Evenflo Vanguard V	1YO	P4	501	636	49
4701	2004 Volvo XC90	Evenflo Vanguard V	3YO	P3	1097	1948	55
4701	2004 Volvo XC90	Graco My CarGo	6YO	P4	825	1243	54**

Appendix C

Test No.	Vehicle	Child Restraint	Dummy	Position	HIC15	HIC36	Chest G
4718	2004 Lexus RX330	Evenflo Vanguard V	3YO	P3	551	882	50
4718	2004 Lexus RX330	Cosco Alpha Omega	3YO	P4	412	793	43
4719	2004 Nissan Maxima	Evenflo Vanguard V	3YO	P3	421	656	43
4719	2004 Nissan Maxima	Britax Express ISOFIX	3YO	P4	404	606	41
4723	2004 Mitsubishi Endeavor	Evenflo Vanguard V	3YO	P3	440	694	54
4723	2004 Mitsubishi Endeavor	Britax Roundabout	3YO	P4	588	889	47
4731	2004 Nissan Quest	Evenflo Vanguard V	3YO	P3	489	781	40
4731	2004 Nissan Quest	Cosco Comfort Ride	3YO	P4	274	553	38
4775	2004 Pontiac Grand Prix	Evenflo Vanguard V	3YO	P3	286	533	37
4775	2004 Pontiac Grand Prix	Century 1500 STE	3YO	P4	342	583	41
4776	2004 Ford Taurus	Evenflo Vanguard V	3YO	P3	257	472	40
4776	2004 Ford Taurus	Graco Treasured CarGo	6YO	P4	1021	1396	58
4798	2004 Acura MDX	Evenflo Vanguard V	3YO	P3	374	580	50
4798	2004 Acura MDX	Evenflo Victory V	3YO	P4	344	507	36
4799	2004 Dodge Intrepid	Evenflo Vanguard V	3YO	P3	394	694	40
4799	2004 Dodge Intrepid	Britax Roundabout	3YO	P4	556	791	51
4809	2004 Ford Freestar	Evenflo Vanguard V	3YO	P3	272	607	38
4809	2004 Ford Freestar	Cosco Alpha Omega 5	3YO	P4	351	593	49
4837	2004 Cadillac DeVille	Evenflo Vanguard V	3YO	P3	325	571	40
4837	2004 Cadillac DeVille	Cosco Regal Ride (OS)	3YO	P4	411	766	41
4838	2004 Jeep Liberty	Evenflo Vanguard V	3YO	P3	379	819	42
4838	2004 Jeep Liberty	Century 1500 STE	3YO	P4	328	666	43
4846	2004 Toyota Sienna	Evenflo Vanguard V	3YO	P3	369	676	41
4846	2004 Toyota Sienna	Britax Roundabout	3YO	P4	319	705	40
4854	2004 Suzuki Aerio	Evenflo Vanguard V	3YO	P3	587	793	56
4854	2004 Suzuki Aerio	Britax Roundabout	3YO	P4	497	729	68
4855	2004 Toyota Solara	Evenflo Vanguard V	3YO	P3	421	625	47
4855	2004 Toyota Solara	Britax Roundabout	3YO	P4	537	716	51
4863	2004 Chevrolet Malibu	Evenflo Vanguard V	3YO	P3	712	1027	53
4863	2004 Chevrolet Malibu	Britax Roundabout	3YO	P4	634	830	52
4864	2004 Mazda 3	Evenflo Vanguard V	3YO	P3	250	418	54
4866	2004 Mitsubishi Galant	Evenflo Vanguard V	3YO	P3	459	710	52
4867	2004 Acura TL	Evenflo Vanguard V	3YO	P3	423	646	47
4867	2004 Acura TL	Britax Roundabout	3YO	P4	439	710	48

Appendix C

Test No.	Vehicle	Child Restraint	Dummy	Position	HIC15	HIC36	Chest G
4871	2004 Toyota Camry	Evenflo Vanguard V	3YO	P3	507	765	50
4871	2004 Toyota Camry	Britax Roundabout	3YO	P4	645	906	52
4872	2004 Hyundai XG350	Evenflo Vanguard V	3YO	P3	635	970	55
4872	2004 Hyundai XG350	Britax Roundabout	3YO	P4	777	976	64
4876	2004 Ford F-150 Super Crew	Evenflo Vanguard V	3YO	P3	228	444	38
4876	2004 Ford F-150 Super Crew	Cosco Touriva	3YO	P4	224	445	35
4877	2004 Hyundai Elantra	Evenflo Vanguard V	3YO	P3	543	754	61
4878	2004 Lincoln LS	Evenflo Vanguard V	3YO	P3	448	641	39
4878	2004 Lincoln LS	Britax Roundabout	3YO	P4	525	816	50
4881	2004 Acura TSX	Evenflo Vanguard V	3YO	P3	344	529	52
4881	2004 Acura TSX	Cosco Touriva	3YO	P4	400	624	45
4887	2004 Suzuki Forenza	Evenflo Vanguard V	3YO	P3	641	916	56
4890	2004 Ford F-150 Excab	Evenflo Vanguard V	3YO	P3	388	605	43
4890	2004 Ford F-150 Excab	Cosco Touriva OS	3YO	P4	254	482	40
4893	2004 Toyota Rav4	Evenflo Vanguard V	3YO	P3	939	1131	63
4899	2004 Chevrolet Colorado	Evenflo Vanguard V	3YO	P3	778	1249	52
4899	2004 Chevrolet Colorado	Evenflo Vanguard OS	3YO	P4	526	946	48
4901	2004 Lexus ES330	Evenflo Vanguard V	3YO	P3	463	721	51
4901	2004 Lexus ES330	Britax Roundabout	3YO	P4	1011	1268	50
4917	2004 Chevrolet Aveo	Evenflo Vanguard V	3YO	P3	329	603	45
4918	2004 GMC Envoy XUV	Evenflo Vanguard V	3YO	P3	*	*	40
4918	2004 GMC Envoy XUV	Cosco Alpha Omega 5	3YO	P4	499	739	38
4923	2004 Cadillac SRX	Evenflo Vanguard V	3YO	P3	739	739	55
4923	2004 Cadillac SRX	Century 1500 STE	3YO	P4	607	1110	50
4927	2004 Dodge Durango	Evenflo Vanguard V	3YO	P3	556	908	48
4927	2004 Dodge Durango	Century 1500 STE	3YO	P4	268	506	48
4930	2004 Toyota Highlander	Evenflo Vanguard V	3YO	P3	614	1000	64
4930	2004 Toyota Highlander	Britax Roundabout	3YO	P4	642	1107	57
4931	2004 Saturn Vue	Evenflo Vanguard V	3YO	P3	433	735	44
4931	2004 Saturn Vue	Cosco Alpha Omega 5	3YO	P4	421	661	50
4933	2004 Toyota Prius	Evenflo Vanguard V	3YO	P3	805	1162	60
4936	2005 Chrysler Town & Country	Evenflo Vanguard V	3YO	P3	531	812	48
4936	2005 Chrysler Town & Country	Century 1500 STE	3YO	P4	699	1050	49
4952	2005 Ford Escape	Evenflo Vanguard V	3YO	P3	532	845	51

Appendix C

Test No.	Vehicle	Child Restraint	Dummy	Position	HIC15	HIC36	Chest G
4952	2005 Ford Escape	Britax Galaxy	3YO	P4	403	693	46
4953	2004 Volkswagen Touareg	Evenflo Vanguard V	3YO	P3	1188	1188	57
4953	2004 Volkswagen Touareg	Safety 1st Comfort Ride	3YO	P4	446	786	45
4960	2004 Infiniti FX35/45	Evenflo Vanguard V	3YO	P3	414	712	42
4960	2004 Infiniti FX35/45	Century 1500 STE	3YO	P4	484	918	49
4985	2005 Chevrolet Equinox	Evenflo Vanguard V	3YO	P3	424	765	43
4985	2005 Chevrolet Equinox	Britax Wizard	3YO	P4	341	617	39
5037	2004 Toyota 4Runner	Evenflo Vanguard V	3YO	P3	446	810	49
5037	2004 Toyota 4Runner	Cosco Touriva OS	3YO	P4	366	741	49
5047	2004 Kia New Spectra	Evenflo Titan V	3YO	P3	535	783	59
5052	2004 Dodge Ram 1500	Evenflo Vanguard V	3YO	P3	695	1255	40
5052	2004 Dodge Ram 1500	Britax Express ISOFIX	3YO	P4	548	933	41
5092	2004 Volvo S40	Evenflo Vanguard V	3YO	P3	1249	1473	73
5092	2004 Volvo S40	Graco My CarGo	6YO	P4	1161	1561	60

* Data Channel Failed
** Data Spike Manually Removed